D1552808

CONTENTS

HINDUISM

teachings, sources, & practices

Edited by
Michael S. Russo

SophiaOmni

ISBN - 978-1547215720

SophiaOmni

Visit our website at:
www.sophiaomni.org

INTRODUCTION

"Truth is One. The wise call it by different names."

Rig Veda 1.164.46

With over one billion followers, Hinduism is the third largest religion in the world after Christianity and Islam. It is also the dominant religion in India. Over 83% of Indians—as many as 700 million people—identify as Hindu. There are also another 80 million Hindus scattered around the world, over 2 million of whom live in the United States.

Hinduism is generally regarded as the oldest living religion in the world, having its origins with the Aryan migrations to India that began almost 4000 years ago. There are those who argue, however, that it should actually be considered the youngest major religion in the world, since it was only in the 19th century that the many disparate spiritual traditions of India began to collectively be referred to as "Hinduism." Prior to this, members of these assorted traditions would probably not have even recognized themselves as belonging to the same religion.

The name "Hindu" itself is of Indo-Aryan origin and is derived from "*Sindhu*"—a word referring to the Indus River. As Zaehner points out, the term simply means Indian. "Hinduism is thus the '-ism' of the Indian people."[1] It was actually the British during their colonization of the Indian subcontinent who began to use the word "Hindu" (or "Hindoo") to refer to those inhabitants of India not practicing Islam, Christianity, Jainism, or Buddhism. So Hinduism historically has been defined by what it is not. Start with the nation of India, subtract the practices and beliefs of those members of the faiths previously listed, and what remains is Hinduism... more or less.

So much for the dry facts about Hinduism. From this point on, the going gets a bit trickier, since Hinduism in many respects is almost totally unique among the major religious traditions of the world. Abraham is recognized as the founder of Judaism, Jesus of Christianity, Mohammed of Islam, and Siddhartha Gautama of Buddhism. But who, you may ask, is the founder of Hinduism? The answer is nobody. Unlike the rest of the world's major religious traditions, Hinduism has no single historical founder. It also has no single doctrinal texts like the Bible or the Koran that are considered authoritative and no single hierarchical body to clarify matters of doctrinal dispute.

Identifying essential beliefs of this tradition, likewise, is not quite as easy as it is for other faiths. If you ask a Christian, Jew, Muslim, or Buddhist to identify the basic tenets of their faith, you'll probably get more or less the same answer from most members within the same faith tradition. Ask Hindus this same question and you're in for trouble. There are Hindus who have a radically monistic view of reality (there is only one true reality) and those who are radically dualistic (there are multiple realities). There are Hindus who believe in a personal deity and those who don't. There are Hindus who believe in one God and Hindus who believe in many gods. There are Hindus who believe the path to ultimate liberation comes from living a life of intense devotion to gods or a god and those who passionately espouse other—sometimes contradictory—paths to the same end.

In a sense we should probably speak of many different "Hinduisms" and recognize that there can be as wide a variety of manifestations of Hinduism as there are practicing Hindus. This is essentially the approach that Allie M. Frazier takes when she describes Hinduism as "the whole complex of events, beliefs, practices and institutions that have appeared in India from the time of the ancient Vedas until the modern age."[2] This sort of approach has the advantage of being inclusive, but is probably too broad to be useful in delimiting any sort of reasonable field of inquiry.

A more practical starting point for discussing the essential features of Hinduism would be to look at how Hindus define themselves. Hindus, in fact, refer to their own tradition, not as Hinduism, but as *sanātana dharma*. *Sanātana* can mean either "universal" or "eternal." *Dharma* can mean, "truth," "reality," or "law" (as it is expressed in sacred texts), depending upon how it's used. "Universal truth" probably comes closest to capturing the meaning of the term, since it suggests certain transcendent "truths" in the tradition that bind all—or at least most—Hindus together.

So far, so good. But what are these unifying truths?

For one thing most Hindus—though certainly not all—refer back to the four Vedas as the main body of sacred literature. The Vedas probably shouldn't be considered the Bible of Hinduism, since Hindus no longer worship many of the gods described in them or practice the sort of sacrifices that these texts advocate. The Vedas however, are generally regarded as the foundational works of the Hindu tradition and therefore are accorded a fairly exalted status by most Hindus that other Hindu works simply don't have. So any legitimate study of Hindu thought has to begin by examining the central ideas contained in these ancient texts.

There are also some essential concepts that most Hindus share. These include *samsara* (reincarnation), *karma* (the belief that one's present situation in life is the result of past actions in past lives and that our present actions will affect our situation in future lives), *moksha* (release from the cycle of reincarnation) as the ultimate goal of life, and *dharma* (that such release is achieved by fulfilling one's duty in life). If you ask just about anyone who identifies as a Hindu, most would certainly recognize these as core concepts of their faith tradition.

Why Study Hindu Thought?

So we've now discovered at least a few things that make Hinduism Hinduism. But a question remains as to why anyone would want to study an intellectual tradition that is so ancient and at times so esoteric. After all, this is the 21st century and one could argue that, if we want answers to the perplexing problems that face our species today, science and contemporary philosophy can probably provide all the answers that we need.

The facile response to this objection is that any religion that has millions of adherents worldwide and which has had such an enormous impact on human spiritual and intellectual development is probably worthy of studying for its own sake. The same, of course, would be true for any of the world's major religions. The fact that so many individuals throughout the course of human history—including some of the most enlightened representatives of our human family—have found meaning, solace, and higher truth in these traditions, to my mind at least, means that there's probably something intrinsically valuable to them that makes them worthy of systematic study.

But Hinduism itself offers a particularly rich and varied intellectual tradition that makes it stand apart even from among the other great religious traditions of the world. Long before philosophers in the West began to rationally inquire about the nature of reality, sages in the Indus Valley were already deeply involved in such investigations. In works like the *Upanishads*, Indian thinkers were struggling with questions like: Is there a Self? If so, what is the nature of this Self? And what happens to the Self after death? These are questions, of course, that continue to confront and perplex us even today. The philosophical traditions of India that began in Vedic times and which continue through the present are second to none in their levels of sophistication and complexity in addressing such questions and their answers are relevant even today. That fact also makes them worthy of systematic study.

Finally, Hinduism is probably the most tolerant religious tradition that has ever existed. In general, Hindus tend to be completely undogmatic, recognizing a plurality of ways to understand reality and to achieve liberation. In the late 19th century, this embrace of pluralism was noted by the Victorian scholars who had begun to study and translate the works of ancient India. As Monier-William wrote in 1891,

> ...Hinduism has something to offer which is suited to all minds. Its very strength lies in its infinite adaptability to the infinite diversity of human characters and human tendencies. It has a highly spiritual and abstract side suited to the metaphysical philosopher—its practical and concrete side suited to the man of affairs and the man of the world—its aesthetic and ceremonial side suited to the man of poetic feeling and imagination—its quiescent and contemplative side suited to the man of peace and lover of seclusion....[I]t holds out the right hand of brotherhood to nature-worshiper, demon-worshiper, animal-worshiper, tree-worshiper, fetish-worshiper.[3]

What Monier-Williams described in the 19th century is equally true in India today. Go to just about any Indian city today and you'll see devotees of Shiva or Kali worshipping next to Vedantists. A Hindu temple might be located just down the street from a Muslim mosque or Christian church. While conflict between members of different faith traditions certainly exists in India—as it does in every society—the spiritual "live-and-let-live" attitude that is characteristic of much of Indian society is also representative of matters of faith.

This welcoming attitude towards different faith traditions is perhaps best reflected in the writing of the 19th century Hindu thinker, Swami Vivekananda. "Seeing that we are so various in our natures," he reflected, "the same method can scarcely be applied to any two of us in the same manner. We have idiosyncrasies in our minds, each one of us; so the method ought to be varied....If there were only one method to arrive at the truth, it would be death for everyone who is not similarly constituted. Therefore the methods should be various."[4] Just as different people need different diets to have their appetites satisfied, so too did Vivekananda believe that we need different religious beliefs and practices to satisfy our deeper spiritual longings.

Compare this sort of joyful embrace of religious pluralism to the somewhat less tolerant attitude towards others faiths that we find in other religious traditions. To one degree or another, adherents of Christianity,

Judaism, and Islam all believe that their faith represents the only legitimate way to attain salvation (understood almost exclusively as achieved
through union with a personal God). As a result, it's often the case that
anyone who takes a different path is in mortal error and must be considered
an "infidel," "heretic," or "apostate," and treated accordingly. The results
have been centuries of sectarianism, dogmatism, and conflict, culminating
in endless hostility between Jews and Muslims, Muslims and Christians,
and among the liberal and conservative factions of each of these faiths.

It would seem that there's a lot we can learn from Hinduism about how
to get along more peacefully with one another in the 21st century.

About This Text

Given that we are examining a 4000 year old religious tradition—and one
that has an enormous amount of variety both in its essential teachings and
in the way those teachings are lived out in daily life—it is basically impossible to do justice to Hinduism in a single text on the subject. The approach
that we'll take in this text is fairly modest and eminently pragmatic in
scope. The title of this text—*Hinduism: Teachings, Sources, and Practices*—should give some idea of what its focus will be.

First of all, this is a text primarily aimed at those with little or no prior
background in Hindu thought. As such, I make no attempt to try to be
totally comprehensive or to provide a sweeping historical survey of Hinduism that one can find in many other texts. Instead, I'll be focusing primarily on examining Hindu thought in light of the four main subdivisions
of Hindu spirituality that have come down to us through the centuries.
These are known as the "Four Yogas"—namely, Jnana Yoga (The Yoga
of Self-Knowledge), Bhakti Yoga (The Yoga of Devotion), Karma Yoga
(The Yoga of Selfless Action) and Raja Yoga (the Yoga of Meditation).
The advantage of this approach is that it allows us to examine the rich
diversity of Hinduism without getting lost in the thicket of centuries of
fairly complex thought. Unfortunately, this selective approach necessarily
means that some important philosophical and religious traditions that have
helped to shape the development of Indian thought will have to be glossed
over. Those seeking a broader perspective on this topic would be advised
to read some of the works listed in the "For Further Reading" section at the
end of this text.

Second, it's my firm conviction that to understand a philosophical or
religious tradition in depth it is necessary to study the original sources
of that tradition. Of course, there are so many spiritual, ritualistic, and
philosophical texts that comprise the Hindu tradition that once again it is
necessary to be selective. In adapting or translating these texts, I've aimed

primarily at readability rather than exacting fidelity to the primary sources. The aim is to give the reader a flavor for these original texts without the confusion that might come from including obscure references or overly technical jargon. If the selections in this text whet your appetite to explore original sources in greater depth, once again I strongly encourage you to investigate some of the primary source works listed at the end of this text.

A final goal of this text is to try to capture the flavor of Hindu thought in both its theoretical and its practical dimensions. Like all the major religions of the world, Hinduism represents not just a set of beliefs, but also traditional practices that enable these beliefs to be lived out in the real world. The goal of Hinduism is liberation or *moksha*. But no one ever became liberated simply by studying ideas in a book—no matter how profound that book might be. Each chapter, therefore, ends with opportunities to engage in some selective Hindu spiritual practices like mantra recitation, meditation, yogic breathing, and Vedantic Self-affirmation that have been an important part of Hinduism throughout the ages. These practices, of course, are not for everyone. Those interested solely in a theoretical understanding of Hinduism should feel perfectly free to skip these sections.

What I think that you'll discover by exploring the rich panorama of Hindu thought and practice is that this ancient and venerable religion has something significant to offer spiritual seekers even in the 21st century. We are all looking for self-realization, enlightenment, or salvation in one form or another. Quite often however, we look in the wrong places. What we have in Hinduism is a well-honed set of teachings that speak to the most fundamental existential questions of human beings—Who are we? Why are we here? And where are we ultimately heading?—and provides answers to these questions that can speak to just about every type of person.

In this sense Hinduism can be considered the world's ultimate perennial philosophy.

NOTES

1. R. C. Zaehner. *Hinduism* (Oxford: Oxford University Press, 1966): 1.
2. Allie M. Frazier. *Hinduism* (Philadelphia: Westminster Press, 1969): 5.
3. Monier Monier-William. *Brahmanism and Hinduism*. 4th ed. (New York: Macmillan and Co., 1891): xi.
4. Swami Vivekananda. *Complete Works*. Vol. 4 (Hollywood, CA: Vedanta Press, 1977-1984): 16.

1
ORIGINS OF HINDUISM: THE VEDAS

We've seen that Hinduism as a religion was not founded by any particular individual. Instead, it emerged over many centuries, combining the beliefs of the indigenous population of the Indus Valley along with the myths and rituals brought to India by the Aryans. Before we can even begin to discuss some of the main beliefs that underlie Hindu thought, then, we'll first have to explore the origins of this religion as it arose during the second millennium BCE.

The Rise of Indus Valley Civilization

There is evidence that human beings began to establish themselves in communities in the Indus Valley region of northern India from as early as 3,200 BCE. Around 2500 BCE, a technologically advanced society was developed by a people known as the Dravidians, whose descendants later migrated to Southern India. These early inhabitants of the Indus Valley built major urban centers in what is today Northern India and Pakistan that were probably among the most sophisticated in the world at the time. Dravidian cities like Mohenjo-Daro and Harappa included features such as brick buildings, multistory dwellings, running water, and modern-like sewerage systems.

Despite the advances of Dravidian civilization, these early inhabitants of the Indus Valley were eventually displaced by another group of people known as the Aryans (literally "noble people"). The Aryans were Indo-European herders and nomads who originated from the steppes in Central Asia. Between 5000 and 3000 BCE, the Aryans moved into Eastern Europe and Northern Iran, and from there advanced into India around 1700 BCE.

Traditionally, it was believed that the lighter-skinned Aryans displaced darker-skinned Dravidians through conquest and plunder. The evidence for this comes from the hymns of the *Rig Veda*, which speaks of battles that destroyed the walled cities of the pre-Aryan inhabitants of the Indus Valley. Today there is a debate over whether there really was an Aryan invasion or just a long, steady migration. Some historians now believe that, rather than being conquered, the original Dravidians experienced an ecological crisis—perhaps severe flooding—that forced them to abandon their urban settlements.

The culture established by the Aryan people is described in great detail in the Vedas. The Aryans were a pastoral, nomadic people whose culture was actually believed to have been far less advanced than that of the Dravidian people that they displaced. Eventually, the Aryans settled down and developed their own kingdoms that shared a common language (Sanskrit) and similar cultural features: a caste-based social organization, agricultural economy, and religion based upon sacrifice.

The original language of the Aryans—Indo-European—would eventually provide a linguistical link amongst India, the Middle East, and Europe. In India, this language would become the Sanskrit of the Vedas, but with Aryan migrations westward, it would eventually become the root mother tongue of other languages was well. The ancient Greeks, Romans, Celts, Slavs, and Germans, as well as the people of Iran (a word derived from Aryan) and Afghanistan, were all of Aryan descent. It is for this reason that one often finds surprising similarities in the languages of these diverse nations.

Once settled in India, the Aryans imposed their own social order upon the people they conquered. One aspect of this Aryan influence was in the imposition of a caste system, which influenced all aspects of life in India—economic, social, religious, and political. Upon entering a particular caste, there was no opportunity to escape from it. One labored according to one's caste and married according to one's caste. At the very top of this caste system were members of the priestly caste (*Brahmins*). The reason that they were considered so important in Vedic society was that they controlled the sacred rites and rituals that enabled human beings to appease the gods through appropriate sacrifices. Just below the Brahmins were the warriors (*Kshatriyas*), who protected the society. The Merchants (*Vaishyas)* were involved in trade and business. The peasants (*Shudras*) were serfs who worked the lands of others and who were believed to have been non-Aryans (e.g., the original Dravidians). Outside of the caste system entirely were the Untouchables (*Dalits*), who were considered unclean, and did only the dirtiest work (cleaning toilets, sweeping streets, tanning animal hides).

The primary manner of worship for the Aryans was sacrifice (*yajña*). As nomadic peoples, the Aryans didn't build temples to their gods, but rather offered sacrifices to them on altars built in open places. Fires would be lit and offerings to the gods thrown into them. The Aryans commonly sacrificed animals, but also milk, butter, meats, and grains—basically anything that would be considered of value to the owner. The most elaborate of these sacrifices was what was known as the horse sacrifice. Because of the expense involved, this sort of sacrifice was probably limited to Aryan rulers, and its aim seems to have been to aid a ruler in expanding his territory. These sorts of sacrifices, while central to Vedic religion, would eventually become far less prominent in later Hinduism, when the practice *ahimsa* (non-violence) that emerged out of Buddhism and Jainism would come to exert a greater influence on Hindu thought.[1]

The Vedas

The Vedas are some of the oldest religious texts in the history of mankind and are considered to be the most sacred books in Hinduism. Although these texts were only formally compiled around 1,500 BCE, the earliest portions of them may in fact date to as early as 1,700 BCE.

The word Veda is derived from the Sanskrit root "vid," which means "to know." This is the same source of the English word "vision" and "video." But the kind of knowledge that the Vedas represent is different from our regular human knowledge, according to Hindus. All Hindu literature can basically be divided into two categories: *sruti* ("what is heard") and *smriti* ("what is remembered"). The Vedas are part of the first category of works which were said to be divinely inspired words as conveyed to *rishis* (human sages or seers). All other Hindu sacred texts, no matter how important or influential they might be, fall into the second category—works produced by human beings, the goal of which traditionally was seen as helping to illuminate the insights of the Vedas.

The Vedas were the result of centuries of oral tradition. They were meant to be passed down from a master to a disciple, memorized with the help of elaborate mnemonic techniques, and recited during ceremonies. Sanskrit, the language of these texts, was regarded by the Aryans as a holy language. The word "Sanskrit" itself means "perfect."

There are four main Vedas: The *Rig Veda* (The Book of Mantra) is the earliest and most important of the Vedas. It is a collection of 1,028 Vedic Sanskrit hymns associated with sacrifices to various gods. These hymns were designed to be chanted aloud by Brahmin priests during religious rites. The term "*rig*" comes from the Sanskrit term "*re*," meaning to praise. The *Sama Veda* (The Book of Song) is a collection of liturgical songs or mantras derived from the *Rig Veda*. The *Yajur Veda* (The Book of Ritual) served as a ritualistic guide for priests. It is comprised of a series of sacrificial formulas (*yajus*) that priests would recite while offering sacrifices. The *Artharva Veda* (The Book of Spells) was composed much later than the other three Vedas and consists of magical spells and charms.

Each Veda consists of four main parts: the *Samhitas* (hymns in praise of various deities), the *Aranyakas* (texts on rituals, ceremonies, and sacrifices), the *Brahmanas* (commentaries on rituals), and the *Upanishads* (philosophy).

The point of all these works was to provide Brahmin priests with the sacred texts necessary to perform ritual sacrifices (*yajna*) properly. The gods were seen as controlling the mysterious and often dangerous forces of nature. The various prayers and rituals of the Vedas were the means whereby the people could get the gods to protect them from harm or provide them with the good things they wanted in life (e.g., wealth, a suitable mate, healthy children).

Many of these sacrifices were quite complex and specific details about what specific rituals in what conditions and in what manner needed to be performed were spelled out in detail in the Vedas:

> Many of the ritualistic observances...required the help of a large number of priests, and large quantities of butter, rice, milk, animals, etc. They had to be performed with the most elaborate details from day to day, for months together and sometimes even for ten or twelve years; and it was enjoined that all observances should be performed in exact accordance with the prescriptions laid down in Brahmana literature. Even the slightest inaccuracy or the most trifling in exactness would be sufficient to spoil the entire effect of the sacrifice. But if the sacrifices were performed with the strictest accuracy, then the material advantages for which they were performed were bound to come regardless of the good will or the ill will of the gods to whom the prayers were offered....The idea of sacrifice is entirely different from anything found in other races. For the Vedic people, the sacrifices were more powerful than the gods. The gods could be pleased or displeased; if the sacrifices were duly performed the prayers were bound to be fulfilled.[2]

Naturally, the incredible specificity of the rites performed assured that priests had a central role in Vedic religion. For this reason, the religious tradition that arose out of the Vedas is often referred to as "Brahmanism" rather than Hinduism per se.

The Vedic Gods (Devas)

Of the 1028 hymns in the *Rig Veda*, the vast majority are dedicated to specific Hindu gods (*devas*, literally, "the shining ones"). Most of these gods are personifications of natural elements: fire, winds, sun, rain, etc. Like most primitive peoples the Aryans believed that the forces of nature were controlled by the gods, who needed to be continually appeased. Since the number of gods addressed in the *Rig Veda* is staggering, we'll limit ourselves to the most prominent.

The god who receives the most attention in the Vedas is Indra—the god of the heavens, of the thunderbolt, and of the clouds and rains. In the *Rig Veda* over 250 hymns are specifically addressed to him. His strength and sexual prowess was said to be so great that he is often symbolically associated with the bull. He is often depicted holding a trident, symbolizing his sovereignty over the world. It was Indra who was said to be the bringer of the monsoons—destroyers of drought—upon which all life in India depends. Indra is also considered important because he conquered Vitra—the personification of evil.

After Indra, the god who is mentioned next most often is Agni—the personification of the sacrificial fire. ("Agni" has the same root as the word "ignite" in English.) Fire was extremely important in Vedic rituals, so it's not surprising that Agni would be involved frequently in the Vedas. In fact, almost 200 hymns in the *Rig Veda* are dedicated to this deity, including the opening hymn of that text (Book 1, Hymn 1). The Aryans considered Agni to be a messenger between humans and the gods.

Varuna was responsible for maintaining the cosmic law (*rita*), which regulates all the activities of this world. He is regarded as the lord of human morality and is responsible for ensuring that there is no violation of human or divine laws.

Soma is the name of a god associated with the effects of a drug by the same name that was used in copious amounts by Brahmins during sacrifices. The drug was derived from unknown plants that grew wild in the mountainous countryside. Supposedly Soma expanded consciousness and produced states of ecstasy in those that partook of it—most notably Brahmin priests who used it to communicate directly with the gods.

Prajapati ("Lord Of Beings") is also known as Purusha. He is the Primordial Man, who sacrifices himself to create the universe. The supreme creator in the Vedas, he is considered the source of all things (including all other gods. Eventually he would become Brahman—the Absolute—in later Hindu thought.

Other deities described in the Rig Veda are connected with the elements—Surya, the sun god and Usas, the goddess of dawn.

It should be noted that the translation of the Sanskrit *devas* as gods is problematic because several of these hymns are addressed to the One or the Supreme *deva*, and that designation is given to different *devas* in different hymns. Although in one sense the Vedas are clearly polytheistic, emphasizing devotion to numerous "deities," the term "polytheism" is perhaps too simplistic as it is typically applied to these works. By the early 7th century BCE, there was already developing in Hinduism the idea that the numerous gods of the Vedas were actually manifestations of a single supreme God. In the *Brihadaranyaka Upanishad* 3.9.1, for example, we read the following exchange between the teacher Yajnavalkya and his pupil:

> Then Vidagdha Sakalya asked: "How many gods are there, O Yajnavalkya?" He replied…, "As many as are mentioned in the Instruction of the hymn to all the Gods—namely, three and three hundred, three and three thousand.
>
> "Yes," he said, and asked again: "How many gods are there really, O Yajnavalkya?"
>
> "Thirty-three," he said.
>
> "Yes," he said, and asked again: "How many gods are there really, O Yajnavalkya?"
>
> "Six," he said.
>
> "Yes," he said, and asked again: "How many gods are there really, O Yajnavalkya?"
>
> "Three," he said.
>
> "Yes," he said, and asked again: "How many gods are there really, O Yajnavalkya?"
>
> "Two," he said.
>
> "Yes," he said, and asked again: "How many gods are there really, O Yajnavalkya'"
>
> "One and a half," he said.
>
> "Yes," he said, and asked again: "How many gods are there really, O Yajnavalkya?"
>
> "One," he said.[3]

Thus, by the time of the *Upanishads* at least, a sort of "pantheistic monotheism" had become common in early Indian thought.[4]

 Selection 1.1 — The Pantheon of the Gods

Vedic Creation Myths

The earliest question in the development of any religious tradition is why is there something rather than nothing? To put this another way, how did the universe and everything in it come into being? This is still a question that intrigues us today, although in the 21st century we tend to look to science to provide the answer. Primitive peoples, on the other hand, had their own myths to explain the universe. As Klaus Klostermaier notes:

> The Hindu view of the world, like all ancient world views, is a mytho-religious one. It does not derive from experimentally verifiable scientific evidence but superimposes a mythical or religious pattern on the visible world, a pattern that stems from a different layer of consciousness. It is a representation of the universe within and reflects the psychological, metaphysical, and religious structure of the ideas of the people rather than describes factual conditions in the objective cosmos.[5]

All the major religions of the world have their own creation myths—The Bible, for example, has the story of Genesis—and typically the rest of the religion's philosophy is derived from such myths.

The Vedas give us several different and often conflicting creation accounts. To the Western mind this might seem a bit bewildering, but it's not as much of a problem for Hindus. For one thing Hindus generally tend not to read their sacred texts in a literal way, but rather understand the ideas and stories contained within them as reflective of deeper spiritual truths. The creation accounts that you'll be reading should not be taken, therefore, as attempts to offer scientific explanations about how the universe came into being, but rather to provide a variety of ways to think about the place of human beings in the cosmos.

We've seen that sacrifice was central to Vedic religion. So it's not surprising that at least one of these Vedic creation myths—the *Purusha Sakta*—would center around the act of sacrifice. In this account, we read how the universe was created by Purusha, the Cosmic Man, who is described as having a thousand heads, a thousand eyes, and a thousand feet. Purusha creates Virāj ("The Shining One") and together they beget Purusha the Son, who is offered as a sacrifice to the gods. Out of this sacrifice comes the Vedas, horse, cattle goats, and sheep. Out of various parts of the sacrificial victim, the moon, the sun, the sky, the heavens, and the earth are said to have been born, as well as gods such as Indra and Agni. Important in this account is the identity of Purusha with the entire universe ("Purusha alone is all this universe."). Another interesting feature of this myth is the explanation that it gives for the existence of the various social castes in Hindu society, which are also said to have their origin in the sacrifice of Purusha.

An even more colorful creation account is given in the *Brihadaranyaka Upanishad,* where the Self (*Atman*) in the form of primordial being (Purusha) realizes that he's alone and creates a woman out of his body. From their union, human beings are born. The woman attempts to disguise herself in various animal forms (cow, mare, etc.) but he takes on similar forms and produces all of the world's animals. The idea here that is common in Hinduism is that all living things have the same divine source and share in their creator's divinity.

The two creation accounts described above are traditionally mythic in nature. A more philosophical approach is found in *Rig Veda* 10.129 with the the *Nasadiya Sukta*—also known as the Hymn of Creation. The name for this myth comes from the Sanskrit *ná ásat* or "not the non-existent." It is considered a later hymn within the *Rig Veda*, since the thought contained within it seems more in keeping with later Hindu philosophy. The text has been celebrated as one of the earliest accounts of skeptical thought, encouraging Hindu's to question all aspects of their faith. The central question raised in the text is a perennial one in religious thought: how could something (the universe) have sprung out of nothing? The teasing answer that is given is that in the end God alone could answer the question of how the universe came into being.

 Selection 1.2 — Vedic Creation Myths

Charms and Spells: The Artharva Veda

The rituals of the *Rig Veda* were so elaborate and expensive that they were probably reserved for those who were well off. But common people in Vedic times also had need of assistance from the gods. Thus we have the strange Vedic text known as the *Artharva Veda*. Possibly composed as late as 500 BCE, the text contains 732 charms, magic spells, and incantations to produce some desired good (long life or good health, for example) or to counteract diseases and other common afflictions. The spells were meant to be recited either by an individual seeking relief or by a sorcerer on his or her behalf. Priests, however, were not required to be present to render the rituals effective.

Keep in mind that life in primitive society was often harsh. War was a common feature of life and hunger and poverty were a constant threat.

Sickness and disease—the causes of which were unknown in an age before modern medicine—were often attributed to evil spirits or demonic forces against which people needed to protect themselves. With the right incantation or spell, such spirits could be controlled

If this all seems bizarre, it should be noted that in many parts of Europe and the United States, so-called "modern people" have all sorts of rituals to help them deal with sickness, suffering, and adversity. Go to any Catholic Church, for example, and you'll find people lighting votive candles and doing their own incantations to have the saints intercede for them.

One could argue that most contemporary religious traditions represent an often uneasy blending of elaborate rites and rituals performed by priestly classes with a healthy dose of popular religious practices cherished by common people. That's certainly the case in the development of Hinduism, where magical elements not completely dissimilar from those described in the *Artharva Veda* play an important role even today.

 Selection 1.3 — Charms and Spells

NOTES

1. Sen, K.M. *Hinduism* (London: Penguin, 1961): 35.
2. Dasgupta, S.N. *Hindu Mysticism* (Delhi: Motilal Banarsidass, 1927): 5-6.
3. Hume, Robert Ernest. *"Brihadaranyaka Upanishad."* The Thirteen Principle Upanishads (London: Oxford University Press, 1921): 119-120. Translation updated.
4. Sharma, Arvind. *Classical Hindu Thought: An Introduction* (New Delhi: Oxford University Press, 2000): 36.
5. Klostermaier, Klaus K. *A Survey of Hinduism* (Albany: State University of New York Press, 1989): 108.

SOURCES

 **1.1 — Pantheon of the Gods**

Rig Veda

Indra [1.32]

I will proclaim the heroic deeds of Indra, the first that the wielder of the thunderbolt performed. He killed the dragon (Vritra), discharged the waters, and split open the caverns of the lofty mountains.

He slew the dragon lying on the mountain. Tvastar (craftsman of the gods) fashioned the thunderbolt for him. Like bellowing cows, the rushing waters have gone straight down to the ocean.

Greedy like a bull he took the soma for himself, and drank its juices in three ceremonial bowls. The generous one grasped the thunderbolt for his weapon; [and with it] he killed the first-born of the dragons.

Indra, when you killed the first-born of the dragons, and thwarted all the wiles of crafty schemers, at that moment you brought forth, the sun, the sky, and the dawn. Since then, there has been no enemy to challenge you.

With his thunderbolt, Indra killed Vritra, the shoulderless one, his greatest enemy. Like trunks of trees, cut down with an ax, the dragon lies flat upon the earth.

Like a drunken coward Vritra challenged Indra, the mighty overcomer, the drinker of soma to the dregs. He could not endure the onslaught of Indra: he was conquered by him and his nose was smashed.

Footless and handless he battled Indra, who struck him on the neck with his thunderbolt. Like a castrated steer wishing to become a bull, Vritra lay cut up in many places.

As he lay there like a broken reed, the flowing waters rushed over him. Beneath the very feet of those waters, which Vritra in his might had once enclosed, the dragon now lay.

The strength of Vritra's mother (Danu) left, for Indra had cast down his thunderbolt upon her. The mother lay above; the son below. Danu lay down like a cow with her calf.

In the midst of water that never stands still, the body of Vritra lies

---

Arthur Anthony Macdonell. *Hymns of the Rig Veda*. London: Oxford University Press, 1922. Translation updated.

hidden. Into the deep darkness sank the foe of Indra.

Enclosed by demons, guarded by a serpent, the waters stood imprisoned, like cows captured by Pani. Those waters which had been blocked were opened when Indra killed Vritra.

You became like the hair of a horse's tail when Vritra struck you on the mouth. You won the cow, oh brave one; you won the soma. And you released the seven streams to flow in torrents.

Neither lightning, nor thunder, nor mist, nor hailstorm, which Vritra spread around, proved effective when Indra and the dragon fought in battle. The generous god gained victory forever.

Who did you see as the avenger of the dragon, that fear entered your heart when you had killed him? Then you crossed the ninety-nine rivers and the heavens like a frightened eagle.

Indra is king of all that is fixed and moving, of tame and horned beasts, the thunder-wielder. He truly rules as king of busy mortals; as a rim enclosed spokes, so does he encompass all.

Agni [1.1]

I pray to Agni, the household priest, god of the sacrifice, the one who invokes and bestows blessings.

Agni is worthy to be praised by ancient and modern seers. May he to us conduct the gods here.

Through Agni may we gain riches, and day-by-day prosperity; and may we abound with fame and heroic sons.

O Agni, the worship and the sacrifice, which you encompass on every side, go straight to the gods.

May Agni, the invoker, wise and true, of most resplendent fame, come here with the gods.

Whatever good you would bestow on the worshipper of you, through you, O Agni, that comes true.

O Agni, illuminator of darkness, day-by-day we approach you with holy thoughts, bringing homage to you.

—to you, lord of the sacrifice, radiant guardian of the cosmic law (*rita*), growing in your own realm.

O Agni, be easy for us to approach, like a father to his son. Abide with us for our welfare.

Soma [8.48]

Wisely I have partaken of the sweet food that stirs good thoughts, best banisher of care, to which all gods and mortals, calling it honey, come together.

If you have entered within, you shall be Aditi, appeaser of divine wrath. May you, O Indu, enjoying the friendship of Indra, like an obedient mare the pole, advance us to wealth.

We have drunk Soma; we have become immortal; we have gone to the light; we have found the gods. What can hostility now do to us, and what the malice of mortal man, O immortal one?

Do good to our heart when drunk, O Indu; kindly like a father, O Soma, to his son, thoughtful like a friend to his friend, O far-famed one, prolong our years that we may live, O Soma.

These glorious, freedom-giving *drops,* ye have knit me together in my joints like straps on a carriage; let those drops protect me from breaking a leg and save me from disease.

Like fire kindled by friction inflame me; illumine us; make us wealthier. For then, in your intoxication, O Soma, I regard myself as rich. Enter into us for prosperity.

Of you pressed with devoted mind we would partake as of paternal wealth. King Soma, prolong our years as the sun the days of spring.

King Soma, be gracious to us for welfare; we are your devotees: know that. There arise might and wrath, O Indu: abandon us not according to the desire of our foe.

Since you are the protector of our body, O Soma, you as surveyor of men have settled in every limb. If we infringe thine ordinances, then be gracious to us as our good friend, O god, for higher welfare.

I would associate with the wholesome friend who having been drunk would not injure me, O lord of the bays. For the enjoyment of that Soma which has been deposited in us, I approach Indra to prolong our years.

Those ailments have started off, diseases have sped away, the powers of darkness have been affrighted. Soma has mounted in us with might: we have gone to where men prolong their years.

The drop drunk in our hearts, O Fathers, that immortal has entered us mortals, to that Soma we would pay worship with oblation; we would abide in his mercy and good graces.

You, O Soma, uniting with the Fathers, have extended yourself over Heaven and Earth. To you as such, O Indu, we would pay worship with offerings: we would be lords of riches.

You protecting gods, speak for us. Let not sleep overpower us, nor idle talk. We, always dear to Soma, rich in strong sons, would utter divine worship.

You are, O Soma, a giver of strength to us on all sides. You are a finder of light. As surveyor of men, enter us. Do you, O Indu, protect us behind and before with your aids accordant.

Surya (Sun) [1.50]

Aloft his beams now bring the god who knows all creatures that are born, that all may look upon the Sun.

Away like thieves the stars depart, by the dark nights accompanied, at the all-seeing Sun's approach.

His beams, his rays, have shone afar athwart the many homes of men, flaming aloft like blazing fires.

Swift-moving, visible to all, maker of light thou art, O Sun, illuming all the shining space.

You rise toward the host of gods and toward the race of men: toward all, that they may see the heavenly light.

The broad air traversing, the sky, you meet, Sun, the days with nights, seeing all creatures that are born,

The seven bay mares that draw your chariot bring you to us, far-seeing god, O Surya of the gleaming hair.

The Sun has yoked the seven bright mares, the shining daughters of his chariot: with that self-yoking team he speeds.

Athwart the darkness gazing up, to him the higher light, we now have soared to Surya, the god among the gods, the highest light.

Usas (Dawn) [1.113]

This light has come, of all the lights the fairest: the brilliant brightness has been born effulgent. Urged onward for god Savitar's uprising, night now has yielded up her place to morning.

Bringing a radiant calf she comes resplendent: to her the Black One has given up her mansions akin, immortal, following each other, Morning and Night fare on, exchanging colors.

The sisters pathway is the same, unending: taught by the gods alternately they tread it. Fair-shaped, of form diverse, yet single-minded, Morning and Night clash not, nor do they tarry.

Bright leader of glad sounds she shines effulgent: widely she has unclosed for us her portals. Pervading all the world she shows us riches: Dawn has awakened every living creature.

Men lying on the ground she wakes to action: Some rise to seek enjoyment of great riches, some, seeing little, to behold the distant: Dawn has awakened every living creature.

One for dominion, and for fame another; another is aroused for winning greatness; another seeks the goal of varied nurture: Dawn has awakened every living creature.

Daughter of Heaven, she has appeared before us, A maiden shining in resplendent raiment. You sovereign lady of all earthly treasure, auspicious Dawn, shine here today upon us....

 **1.2 — Vedic Creation Myths**

The Primeval Sacrifice (Purusha Sakta)
[Rig Veda 10.90]

Thousand-headed was Purusha, thousand-eyed, thousand-footed. Having covered the earth on all sides, he extended beyond it by the length of ten fingers.

Purusha alone is ALL this—that which has been and that which will be. And he is the lord of immortality, and grows beyond everything by consuming food.

Such is his greatness. And greater indeed is this Purusha. All creatures constitute a fourth of him; three-fourths of him are the immortal in heaven.

With three quarters Purusha rose upward; one quarter of him here came into being again. Then he spread out in all directions into animate and inanimate objects.

From him Viraj (the Shining One) was born; from Virāj Purusha was born again. Being born, he reached behind the earth and also before it.

The gods performed a sacrifice with Purussha as an oblation. The spring was its clarified butter, the summer its fuel, the autumn its oblation.

The sacrificial victim—Purusha—born in the beginning, they sprinkled with sacred water upon the sacrificial grass. With him the gods, the heavenly beings, and the seers [*rishis*] performed the sacrifice.

From that sacrifice completely offered was collected the clotted butter. Then came that the beasts of the air, of the forest, and those of the village.

From that wholly offered sacrifice were born the hymns and the sacred chants; the meters were born from it; the sacrificial formula was born from it.

From that the horses were born and those animals that have two rows of teeth. Cattle were born from that; from that were born goats and sheep.

When they divided Purusha, into how many different portions did they arrange him? What did his mouth become? His two arms? What are his two legs called? His two feet?

His mouth became the Brahmin (priest), his two arms became the Rajanya (warrior), his two legs the Vaishya (merchant); from his two feet the Sudra (peasant) was born.

Arthur Anthony Macdonell. *A Vedic Reader for Students*. Oxford: Clarendon Press, 1919. Translation updated.

The moon was born from his mind; the sun was born from his eye; from his mouth came Indra and Agni; from his breath (*prāna*) the wind was born.

From his navel the air was produced; from his head the sky was evolved; from his two feet the earth, from his ear the four directions. In this way have the worlds been formed.

Seven were the enclosing sticks in this sacrifice, three times seven were the fire-sticks made, when the gods, performing the sacrifice, bound Purusha as the victim.

With the sacrifice the gods sacrificed to the sacrifice. these were the first norms (*dharma*) of sacrifice. These powers reached the heaven where the ancient gods and other beings dwell.

The Creation of the World
[Brihadaranyaka Upanishad 14]

In the beginning this world was Soul (*Atman*) alone in the form of a Person. Looking around, he saw nothing else than himself. He said first: 'I am.' From that arose the name 'I.' Therefore even today, when one is addressed, he says first just 'It is I' and then speaks whatever name he has. Since before (*purva*) all this world he burned up (*ush*) all evils, therefore he is a person (*purusha*). He who knows this, then, burns up him who desires to try to get ahead of him.

He was afraid. Therefore one who is alone is afraid. And he thought to himself: 'Since there is nothing else than myself, of what am I afraid?' Then his fear passed, for of what should he have been afraid? For truly it is from another that fear arises.

But he had no delight at all. For one has no delight when one is alone. He longed for a second person. Since he was as large as a woman and a man together, he caused that Self to split (*pat*) into two pieces, from which arose a husband (*pati*) and a wife (*patnī*). Therefore, this is the reason that Yājñavalkya used to say 'Oneself is like a half-fragment'. Therefore the void that was there is filled by a wife. He copulated with her and from their union human beings were produced.

And she then thought to herself: 'How can he have sexual relations with me after he has produced me from himself? Come, let me hide myself.' She became a cow. But he became a bull and had sex with her and

The Thirteen Principle Upanishads. Trans. Robert Ernest Hume. London: Oxford University Press, 1921. Translation updated.

thus cattle were born. Then she became a mare and he a stallion. She became a female ass and he a male ass. Again he had sex with her and from their union solid-hoofed animals were born. She became a female goat and he a male goat; she a ewe and he a ram. And again he had sex with her, and from their union were born goats and sheep. Thus, indeed, he created all the pairs there are, down to the ants.

He knew: 'I am this creation, for I created it all from myself.' From this all creation arose. Anyone who has this knowledge comes to be in that creation of his.

Then he rubbed. From his mouth as from a vagina and from his hands he created fire (*agni*). Both these (i.e. the hands and the mouth) are hairless on the inside, for the vagina (*yoni*) is hairless on the inside. People say, 'Worship this god! Worship that god!'—one god after another. But each god is his manifestation, for he created all gods. Now, whatever is moist, that he created from semen, and that is Soma. Truly, this whole world is just food and the eater of food.

That was Brahma's super-creation: namely, that he created the gods, his superiors; likewise, that, being mortal, he created the immortals. Therefore was it a super-creation. And those who know this come to be in that super-creation of his.

Nasadiya: The Creation Hymn of Rig Veda
[Rig Veda 10.129]

There was neither being nor non-being then;
there was neither the air nor the heaven which is beyond.
What encompassed all? Where? In whose protection?
Was there water, unfathomably deep?

There was neither death nor immortality then.
There was no distinguishing mark of night or day.
That One breathed, windless, by its own power.
Other than that, nothing else existed then.

In the beginning, darkness was hidden by darkness;
all this was the void with no distinguishing forms.
Coming into being, that One was hidden by the void,
and was generated through the power of heat.

"Nasadiya." Trans. Michael S. Russo.

Desire came upon that One in the beginning—
that was the first seed of mind.
Sages searching their hearts with wisdom
found the bond of being in non-being.

Their cord was extended across:
Was there a below or was there an above?
There were impregnators, there were powers;
there was energy below, there was impulse above.

Who truly knows? Who shall proclaim it here?
Out of what was this creation fashioned? From where did it emanate?
The gods came only after the creation of the universe.
Who then knows the source from which it arose?

From where did this creation arise?
Perhaps it formed itself; perhaps not.
Only the One who looks down from the highest heaven knows…
or perhaps even He does not know.

 ## 1.3 — Charms and Spells

Atharva Veda

Charm Against Poison

The Brahmana was the first to be born, with ten heads and ten mouths. He was the first to drink the soma; that did render poison powerless.

As great as heaven and earth are in extent, as far as the seven streams did spread, so far from here have I proclaimed forth this charm that destroys poison.

The eagle Garutmant did, O poison, first devour you. you did not bewilder him, did not injure him, yes, you did turn into food for him.

The five-fingered hand that did hurl upon you (the arrow) even from the curved bow—from the point of the arrow have I charmed away the poison.

From the point of the arrow have I charmed away the poison, from the substance that has been smeared upon it, and from its plume. From its barbed horn, and its neck, I have charmed away the poison.

Powerless, O arrow, is your point, and powerless is your poison. Moreover of powerless wood is your powerless bow, O powerless arrow!

They that ground the poison, they that daubed it on, they that hurled it, and they that let it go, all these have been rendered impotent. The mountain that grows poisonous plants has been rendered impotent.

Impotent are they that dig you, impotent art you, O plant! Impotent is that mountain height from which this poison has sprung.

Charm Against Mania

Release for me, O Agni, this person here, who, bound and well-secured, loudly jabbers! Then shall he have due regard for your share of the offering, when he shall be free from madness!

Agni shall quiet down your mind, if it has been disturbed! Cunningly do I prepare a remedy, that you shall be freed from madness.

He, whose mind has been maddened by the sin of the gods, or been robbed of sense by the Rakshas, for him do I cunningly prepare a remedy,

"Hymns of the Atharva-Veda." Trans. Maurice Bloomfield. *Sacred Books of the East*. Volume 42. Oxford: Oxford University Press, 1897. Translation updated.

that he shall be free from madness.

May the Apsaras restore you, may Indra restore you, may Bhaga restore you; may all the gods restore you, that you may be freed from madness!

Prayer for Health and Long Life

I release you unto life by means of my offering, from unknown decline, and from consumption. If seizure has caught hold of this person here, may Indra and Agni free him from that!

If his life has faded, even if he has passed away, if he has been brought to the very vicinity of death, I snatch him from the lap of the goddess of destruction: I have freed him unto a life of a hundred autumns.

I have snatched him from death by means of an offering which has a thousand eyes, hundredfold strength, and ensures a hundredfold life, in order that Indra may conduct him through the years across to the other side of every misfortune.

Live thou, thriving a hundred autumns, a hundred winters, and a hundred springs! May Indra, Agni, Savitar, Brihaspati grant you a hundred years! I have snatched him from death with an offering that secures a life of a hundred years.

Enter you, O in-breathing and out-breathing, as two bulls a stable! Away shall go the other deaths, of which, it is said, there are a hundred more!

Remain here, O in-breathing and out-breathing, do not go away from here; do ye care anew to old age his body and his limbs! To old age I make you over, into old age I urge you; may a happy old age guide you! Away shall go the other deaths, of which, it is said, there are a hundred more!

Upon you life unto old age has been deposited, as a rope is tied upon a bull. That death which has fettered thee at thy birth with a firm rope, Brihaspati with the hands of the truth did strip off from thee.

Against Sorcerers and Demons

May this offering carry off the sorcerers, as a river carries foam! The man or the woman who has performed this sorcery, that person shall here proclaim himself!

This sorcerer has come here: receive him quickly! O Brihaspati, put him into subjection; O Agni and Soma, pierce him through!

Slay the offspring of the sorcerer, O soma-drinking Indra, and subject him! Make drop out the farther and the nearer eye of the demon!

Wherever, O Agni Gatavedas, you perceive the brood of these hidden devourers, do you, mightily strengthened by our charm, slay them: slay their families, O Agni, piercing them a hundredfold!

Curse Against One That Practices Hostile Charms

The thousand-eyed curse having yoked his chariot has come here, seeking out him that curses me, as a wolf the house of him that owns sheep.

Avoid us, O curse, as a burning fire avoids a lake! Strike here him that curses us, as the lightning of heaven the tree!

He that shall curse us when we do not curse, and he that shall curse us when we do curse, him do I hurl to death as a bone to a dog upon the ground.

Charm to Secure the Love of a Woman

Obsess after my body, my feet, obsess after my eyes, my thighs! The eyes of you, as you lust after me, and your hair shall be parched with love.

I make you cling to my arm, cling to my heart, so that you shall be in my power, shall come up to my wish!

The cows, the mothers of the ghee, who lick their young, in whose heart love is planted, shall make that woman bestow love upon me!

Charm to Arouse the Passionate Love of a Man

From your head down to your feet do I implant love's longing into you. You gods, send forth the yearning love: may that man burn after me!

Favor this plan, Anumati; fit it together, Akuti! You gods, send forth the yearning love so that man may burn after me!

If you run three leagues away, or even five leagues, the distance coursed by a horseman, from there you shall again return, shall be the father of our sons!

PRACTICES

Vedic Mantra Meditation

Just as there are many different types of Hindus, there are also many different types of spiritual practices that developed in India throughout the centuries. You'll explore several of these as you progress through this text. But meditation is something that most people need to ease into gently. There's nothing worse than joining some meditation class that involves an hour of breath meditation only to find yourself screaming inside, because you were unprepared for the practice.

During the period of the Vedas spiritual practice was not something practiced in monasteries, but was part of the everyday life of householders—ordinary people like you and me with family, social, and economic commitments. What developed was a spiritual practice perfectly in tune with the busy lifestyles of average people. And just like most of us today, householders in Vedic India were probably inundated with distractions and troublesome thoughts that made life less than perfectly tranquil.

Fortunately, the rishis of ancient India developed a practice that could help calm the minds of ordinary people though the use of what is known as a mantra. The word mantra comes from the Sanskrit "*manas*" (mind) and "*tra*" (tool or instrument). Literally, then, a mantra is a verbal instrument to produce something in one's mind (Zimmer, 72).

Technically, a mantra is a spiritual formula that is meant to be repeated inwardly (i.e., silently), while a chant is usually recited aloud, but Vedic mantras functioned essentially as chants. These mantras were meant to be chanted aloud by Brahmin priests as part of their rituals and sacrifices. It was believed that sacred sounds when uttered properly have great spiritual power. Naturally, not just anyone was suited to chant these mantras. To do so required years of learning in order to chant in the proper tone and volume.

Chanting the Gayatri Mantra

One of the most sacred and powerful mantras in the Vedic tradition is called the Gayatri mantra (also known as the Savitri mantra), which is from the *Rig Veda* (Book III, Hymn 62, Verse 10) and has existed in written form for at least 2500 years. Understood literally, it is a prayer for blessing from the sun-god Savitar, but in more general terms is a call for illumination from the Supreme Being. This mantra is typically included as part of the Upanayana ceremony that marked the acceptance of a student by his guru and the beginning of his study of the Vedas. Pious Hindus chant it at least three times a day. It is said to bestow light upon the intellect of those who recite it correctly.

In Sanskrit, the mantra reads as follows:

Om bhur bhuvah svah
Tat savitur varenyam
Bhargo devasya dhimahi
Dhiyo yo nah prachodayat

Although this mantra can be translated in many different ways, this is one possible version:

Om. We meditate upon the transcendent glory
Of the Supreme Divine Being.
May he enlighten our intellects
And bestow upon us true knowledge.

A simpler version reads as follows:

Om. We meditate upon
The excellent glory
Of the Supreme Being,
Who illuminates our minds.

It should be noted that it's believed that to be truly efficacious, Vedic mantras like this one should be repeated in the original Sanskrit. You can find numerous recordings of it on the Internet, if you'd like to try it in its original form. But you can also just chant one of the English versions above, if that's easier for you.

Traditionally, this chant is practiced at dawn or dusk, with the rising or the setting of the sun. This is a formality, though, and you can certainly try it in the morning as soon as you wake up or at night before you go to bed. Typically the Gayatri mantra is chanted 108 times using a mala (a string of wooden meditation beads), but you should feel free to chant it as many times as you'd like.

Chanting Other Vedic Mantras

Gayatri may be the "mother of all mantras," but there are also several other

Vedic chants that are recited frequently in Hindu practice.

Choose one of the following Vedic mantras from the list below. Some of these are more religious in nature than others, so you should choose one that resonates most with your own beliefs. Read over the mantra a few times until you have it fairly well memorized. Then just say the words over and over in your mind until the repetition becomes almost effortless. If distracting thoughts arise as you repeat the mantra in your mind, just ignore them and return to repeating the mantra.

As the mantra moves deeper and deeper into your consciousness, you'll probably notice that both your mind and body become a bit calmer as a result. That's because your mind—perhaps for the first time—is no longer fixated on the endless chatter of thought flowing through it. For some, this is true bliss.

Try devoting five or ten minutes a day to practicing this form of mantra meditation. If you have trouble sleeping try it before going to bed and see if it helps you sleep better. If the Vedic mantras included in this chapter don't resonate with you, you'll find a wider variety of mantras from different religious traditions at the end of Chapter 4.

God is Perfect
Isha Upanishad

God is perfect.
This Universe is also perfect.
If perfection is taken from anything perfect what remains is still perfect.
Let there be peace, peace, peace.

Three Aspirations
Brihadaranyaka Upanishad

Lead me from the unreal to the real.
Lead me from darkness to light.
Lead me from death to immortality.

Universal Peace Prayer
Atharva Veda

Supreme Lord, let there be peace in the sky and in the atmosphere.
Let there be peace in the plant world and in the forests.
Let the cosmic powers be peaceful.

Let the Brahman, the true essence and source of life, be peaceful.
Let there be undiluted and fulfilling peace everywhere.

There is a Light
Chandogya Upanishad

There is a light that shines beyond all things on earth,
beyond all of us, beyond the heavens,
beyond the highest, the very highest heavens.
This is the light that shines in our hearts.

The Universal Prayer
Brihadāraṇyaka Upanishad

May all be prosperous and happy.
May all be free from illness.
May all see what is good in all things.
May no one suffer.
Om peace, peace, peace.

2
Overview of Hindu Thought

What we refer to as "Hinduism" is actually a complex faith divided up into hundreds of different sects with their own particular forms of worship, philosophical traditions, and unique organizational structures. In some ways it is completely wrong to talk about Hinduism as some kind of monolithic religion. As Jeaneane Fowler observes:

> Hinduism is much too broad a phenomenon to be confined to the usual definitions of religion. It represents a whole spectrum of beliefs and practices....Similarly, there are no criteria for establishing *who* is a Hindu because no two Hindus will necessarily think alike; there are no uniformly accepted beliefs, sacraments, rituals, and practices to make this possible....It would, therefore, be more correct to speak of *Hinduisms* than of Hinduism in the singular.[1]

As we saw in the previous chapter, Hinduism is a synthesis of various traditions and practices that developed in India 4000 years ago. As such, Hinduism is a religion that almost maddeningly resists simple classifications.

Despite the differences among Hindus, there are certain shared beliefs that are an essential part of what we generally refer to as Hinduism. The concepts of *Atman*, *karma*, *samsara*, *dharma*, and *moksha* are present in one form or another in all Hindu thought and influenced the development of other Indian traditions such as Buddhism and Jainism.

In this chapter the goal is to shed light on these essential concepts within Hinduism. Keep in mind, however, that there are differences in the way that Hindus understand these concepts. Consequently, the ideas presented in this chapter are an attempt to paint the canvas of Hinduism in very broad strokes to give the kind of general overview of Hindu thought that can serve as a foundation for the topics presented in subsequent chapters.

Major Hindu Deities

There is a plurality of ideas about the nature of God and the gods in Hinduism. As Julius Liper notes, "One may be polytheistic or monotheistic, monistic or pantheistic, even an agnostic, humanist or atheist, and still be considered a Hindu."[2]

Although in general Hindus worship a multiplicity of gods, there is only one Absolute Being. Called Brahman (or alternatively, the Divine or God), this being is seen as the underlying substance of the universe. Everything—plants, rocks, mountains, rivers, and you and me—has its origin in Brahman. Thus, although in one sense Hinduism can be said to be a polytheistic religion because Hindus worship a number of different gods and goddesses, if one considers that all the gods in Hinduism are simply considered manifestations of the Absolute, then the term "polytheism" is too simplistic when applied to Hinduism.

We've spoken in the previous chapter about the pantheon of deities in Vedic Hinduism. But that was just the beginning of the story of the gods of the Hindu religion. Over time, even more divine beings began to be worshipped in the Hindu religion—far too many, in fact, to be described in these pages. These many different gods have their own unique personalities and myths surrounding them and so appeal to the different personalities and temperaments of individual Hindus. For Hindus this plurality of gods is not a problem at all: they all are seen as representing different aspects of Brahman "with form."

Although there are a bewildering variety of gods in Hinduism—supposedly 330 million!—the three main ones are the "trinity" of Brama, Vishnu, and Siva.

Brahma (The Creator) in traditional Hinduism should not be confused with Brahman in Vedic Hinduism. The latter is an impersonal force; Brahma, on the other hand, is a distinct entity. Brahma represents the emanation of Brahman into the realm of creation.

The god of love and forgiveness, Vishnu (The Preserver) is seen as having taken on different avatars (manifestations) throughout the course of human history to help liberate human beings from evil. He is said to have already appeared on earth in nine forms—including Krishna in the *Bhagavad Gita*, Rama, and the Buddha—and will come again one more time to bring the world to an end. His main consort is Lakshmi.

In stark contrast to Vishnu, Shiva (The Destroyer) is the god of death and destruction. Sometimes referred to as the "Lord of the Dance," Shiva is typically depicted dancing—usually while tormenting human beings who have offended him—symbolizing the acts of creation and destruction, birth and death. His popularity in Hindu society may have something to do with the fact that he is also the god of sex and reproduction. In temples dedicated to him one will typically find a lingam—a symbol of the male penis.

Shiva has several different consorts, including Parvati (love), Umma (wife and motherhood), and Kali (death). Kali is a particularly colorful deity, who is often depicted wearing a necklace of skulls or drinking blood. His son is Ganesha, who has the head of an elephant.

Atman (The Self)

We've seen that Hindus believe that Brahman—Absolute Being—exists in all things. It stands to reason, then, that they would also believe that he exists in human beings as well.

Hindus believe that all living things have an eternal soul. In Sanskrit the term that is used is "*Atman*". The term comes from the word "*atma*," which literally means "breath" and is used to describe the true essence of an individual. Common to all orthodox schools of Hinduism is the belief that the essence of a person is not to be found in the body, mind, or ego, but in *Atman*—the Self. As Krishna reminds Arjuna in the *Bhagavad Gita*:

> You were never born; you will never die. You have never changed; you can never change. Unborn, eternal, immutable, immemorial, you do not die when the body dies….as a man abandons worn-out clothes and acquires new ones, so when the body is worn out a new one is acquired by the Self who lives within.[3]

Basically, there are two strains in Hinduism—the monistic and the dualistic—that offer somewhat different accounts of the relationship of *Atman* to Brahman. In general, monism is the theory that only one single reality exists in the universe; while dualism posits the existence of multiple realities.

In monistic Hinduism *Atman* is seen as identical to Brahman. The aim of spiritual practice is to realize this identity. In dualistic Hinduism, on the other hand, *Atman* is seen as part of Brahman, but not identical to it. The aim of spiritual practice is for the self to join with, come to know, or come to love Brahman.

This real, eternal, spiritual Self (*Atman*) is distinct from the temporal body made of matter (*prakriti*). We think of the body as our true selves because of illusion (*maya*). It is this identification of oneself with material reality—particularly with the body—that some Hindu thinkers believe causes us to undergo *samsara* (cycle of rebirth and death).

 **Selection 2.1 — The Origins of the Self**

The Big Problem: Samsara

The basic human problem that all human beings have had to contend with since the development of consciousness is the reality of suffering. "Why do bad things happen to good people?" could be the most fundamental question that human beings have had since the beginning of recorded history. Of course, one could answer this question by simply stating that "stuff happens" (that there is no higher meaning or purpose guiding our lives) or, even worse, that God allows us to suffer unjustly. Neither of these answers of course would have appealed to our early ancestors. Instead, in every major religion of the world, an attempt was made to explain the problem of human suffering while at the same time affirming the justice of God and the fundamental order of the universe. In other words, if suffering exists—and we know it does—then there has to be some higher reason for it.

In Hinduism, the cause of our suffering is related to *samsara*. The term, which literally means "a wandering through," is usually translated as "reincarnation," "rebirth," or "transmigration." Essentially it refers to the belief that our individual lives are caught in ever repeating cycles of birth, death, and rebirth. According to Hinduism, after we die, our soul (*Atman*) will be reborn in another body. In the *Bhagavad Gita*, we read, "As the same person inhabits the body through childhood, youth, and old age, so too at the time of death he attains another body. The wise are not deluded by these changes."[4] Ultimately, it is the way that we live our lives that determines our state in future lives.

Samsara is directly connected to the problem of suffering because it means that we must continue on from one life to the next endlessly and possibly return in a much worse situation. But even if we come back in a better state in the next life there's still no escape from sickness, mental anguish, and death. As long as we continue on the treadmill of *samsara*, in other words, we can never be freed of suffering.

 Selection 2.2 — Reincarnation

The Cause of this Problem: Karma

But what is the cause of *samsara*? The answer, as indicated above, has to do with the performance of specific actions in this life. The Sanskrit term for "action" is *karma*. The "law of *karma*" means that all of our actions "bear fruit"—they have reactions or consequences—either in the present or at some point in the future.

The concept of *karma* was already prevalent in a simplified form in the Vedic society. Vedic faith, according to David Knipe, "presumed human responsibility for ritual actions (*karma*) of sacrifices that recycled cosmic energies and resulted simultaneously in continuous renewal of the world and personal regeneration of the sacrificers….The law of *karma* at that point was concise: ritual work was incumbent upon human beings, and it obtained immediate and apparent cosmic, social, and individual results."[5]

Karma in the Vedic tradition, therefore, specifically referred to actions performed during ritual sacrifices. By the 6th century BCE, however, the concept of *karma* grew beyond mere ritual action to encompass all human action. And this includes not only physical actions, but verbal actions (speech) and mental actions (thought) as well. All our actions, it came to be believed, were capable of producing specific causal reactions.

To put this in popular terms, "What goes around comes around." In brief, good actions were thought to have good consequences, and bad actions to have the opposite effect. This idea makes some intuitive sense, if you look at your own life objectively: When you engage in selfish, petty, or vicious actions, doesn't your life become filled with uneasiness? Don't your relationships become more difficult and filled with conflict? Conversely, during those times when you're capable of behaving compassionately, kindly or generously, doesn't life itself seem more enjoyable? More rewarding? Don't your relationships seem more harmonious?

The temporal effects of *karma* may seem evident, but there's still more to this concept in Hinduism that transcends even this specific life of ours. There's also the belief that *karma* determines the conditions in our next life as well. Again, to put it very simply, those who do good in this life will experience better conditions in the next; those who do bad will experience worse conditions. As we'll see, the ultimate goal is to work off our bad *karma* and to attain liberation thus ending the tragic cycle of rebirth.

 Selection 2.3 — The Nature of Karma

The Solution to this Problem: Following One's Dharma

But how do we know the right way to act so as to generate good *karma*? In Vedic society, as we've seen, the answer was fairly simple: engage in the proper actions involved in ritual sacrifice and you will be doing what's right and the gods will, therefore, be appeased.

As with the concept of *karma*, in later Hindu thought, the idea of living rightly took on a much broader focus: To live rightly, it was believed, we need to follow our particular "*dharma*" (from Sanskrit root "*dhri*," meaning to sustain or preserve). In Hinduism, *dharma* is a fairly ambiguous term that can mean "duty," "virtue, or "morality." In general, *dharma* is considered the power that sustains the universe and human society. It's any action that brings well-being to human beings and leads them to liberation.

So in one sense *dharma* is a universal force. But it is also the case that there are various rules of *dharma* written into the Hindu scriptures that tell people how they should live according to their particular social position in society. One fulfills one's *dharma* by living in accordance with one's caste (*varna*). Thus, brahmins have a different set of duties than do warriors or merchants; householders have a different set of duties than do students or renunciates. The assumption is that one belongs to a specific caste because of actions performed in a previous life. As Thomas Hopkins writes:

> [The] *varnas* were related to [a person's] development through many lives in the course of transmigration. It was assumed that a person belonged to that *varna* for which he was qualified by ability and temperament as a result of his actions in past lives. Birth into a family belonging to a given *varna* was *de facto* evidence of the quality of his past lives. The *dharma* of that birth was the proper recompense for past actions and defined the possibilities for future development. The wise man did not question his birth; he fulfilled his present *dharma*, knowing that it suited his current level of development and would advance him towards his ultimate goal.[6]

Various texts, including the *Laws of Manu*, provided the details of the duties belonging to members of each caste. One major responsibility of members of the "twice-born" castes—Brahmins, warriors, and merchants—was to study the Vedas and to learn important Vedic rituals. Brahmins alone had the responsibility to oversee ritual sacrifices and transmit Vedic knowledge. Members of the peasant caste (*shudras*) were specifically forbidden from studying the Vedas. As Sankara in his commentary on the Vedanta Sutras wrote, "The ears of [the *shudra*] who hears the Veda are to be filled with molten lead and hard resin...For a *shudra* is like a cemetery, therefore the Veda is not to be read in the vicinity of a *shudra*."[7] But *shudras* had their own dharma and that was to serve members of the three upper castes. If they performed their duties diligently, it was believed that they potentially could be reborn into a higher caste in a subsequent life.

One's *dharma*, however, was not simply related to responsibilities within one's caste. Depending upon one's particular stage of life (*asrama*) within that caste—student, household, hermit, or renunciate—one also had particular duties that would change as one passed from one stage of life to another. We'll have more to say about this later.

 ## Selection 2.4 — Origins of Caste-Dharma

The Ultimate Goal: Moksha

We've seen that according to the law of *karma*, one's actions in this life determine one's specific state in the next. For example, if a person has lived a good life, then he might be born into a higher caste in the next life. If, on the other hand, a person has lived a bad life, then he might be reborn into a lower caste. A particularly bad person might be reborn as an animal—potentially even a very lowly animal like a worm—depending upon how severe his offenses were. Those, however, who succeed in working their way up the ladder of *samsara* might eventually return as a brahmin priest or even as a god. The problem is that as long as one is trapped on the wheel of *samsara*, there's never a guarantee that one's future state won't take a turn for the worse.

This is why the ultimate goal of life in Hinduism is not simply to attain the best state of life that one can, but to experience *moksha* or liberation. We definitely shouldn't think of *moksha* as some kind of place that the soul goes after death—like heaven in the Christian tradition. *Moksha* specifically refers to the release of the Self from the cycle of *samsara*. Depending upon the particular tradition in Hinduism, *moksha* can mean different things: (1) the identification of the Self with Brahman; (2) the union of the Self with Brahman; (3) the realization of the unity of all reality. What it means for all Hindus is to be liberated from the confining reality of personhood and freed from the petty dictates of ego and desire. The realization of *moksha* liberates one from *samsara*, ending the cycle of rebirth and suffering.

The Four Stages of Life

The life of an individual in Hinduism is divided into four distinct periods (*asramas*). These stages are connected to the Hindu caste system and apply specifically to the three upper castes or the "Twice-Born"—Brahmins, warriors, and merchants. It should also be noted that these stages apply only to males. Women in traditional Hindu society were expected to stay at home under the protection of the chief male of the household.

The ultimate aim of life for any Hindu, as we've seen, is *moksha* or liberation. What's interesting about the way that these four stages of life are organized is that they don't require complete renunciation—at least not in the earlier stages of life. There's a time and a place when a man is still young to enjoy material wealth (*artha*) and physical pleasures (*kama*), while at the same time fulfilling his duty (*dharma*). But ultimately, as one gets older, there's also the call to regulate these sorts of desires for the sake of attaining liberation (*moksha*). These four—*artha, kama, dharma,* and *moksha*—are often referred to in Hinduism as "the four goals of life" and each is recognized as a perfectly legitimate pursuit. The more mundane human desires for wealth and pleasure, however, are viewed by Hindus as ultimately unsatisfying. As Swami Nikhilananda writes:

> No finite experience can permanently satisfy the craving of the soul…Nevertheless, in the lower stages of evolution, the appetite for material things cannot be ignored. If this appetite is suppressed or inhibited, an unhealthy condition is created affecting both man's body and mind. The Hindu philosophers want us gradually to transform the inclination of the senses, will, and mind, so that they may become man's helpers in the attainment of his spiritual end and not remain his enemies.[8]

The first stage of life is that of the student (*Brahmacarya*). This is a period of formal education, which begins between the ages of eight and twelve and continues until twenty-four. During this period, a student is taught by a guru to prepare for his formal life as a member of one of the higher castes. For Brahmins this entails a detailed study of the Vedas and learning to perform rites. Because the student is unmarried, he is expected to remain celibate during these years.

In the second stage of life one becomes a householder (*Grihastha*). This is the period of marriage and raising a family. One thing that is evident from the description of the life of a householder is that Hinduism is anything but an otherworldly religion. During this stage, it is completely appropriate for a householder to be focused on the attainment of material success and wealth (*artha*) and to enjoy physical pleasures (*kama*), including sexual activity with his spouse.

After a man's children have grown up and have established families of their own, a person's duties as a householder formally end. A man is then encouraged to retreat from both family and social life, becoming a hermit or forest dweller (*Vanaprastha*). As the Laws of Manu state: "…when a householder sees that he is wrinkled and grey, and (when he sees) the children of his children, he should take himself to the wilderness." During this stage, a man takes up pilgrimages and religious observances, and engages in meditation. Although it was common to go off alone, wives occasionally did join their husbands as forest dwellers.

During the final stage of life, a man renounces the world completely—including his wife and his formal religious observances and devotes himself exclusively to seeking *moksha*. At this point he becomes a *sadhu* or *sannyasin*—a holy man or wandering hermit. He lives alone, without a home, and depends upon donations for food.

Although these stages might have been followed more closely in the past, today in most Hindu families, the emphasis is placed more intensely—and perhaps almost exclusively—on the preparation to become a householder and the responsibilities that lifestyle entails.

 Selection 2.5 — The Four Stages of Life

The Four Yogas

Although in the West the term "yoga" is most closely identified with the tradition of Hatha Yoga, in Hinduism, the term has a much broader connotation, and refers to various traditions, philosophies, and practices that have developed within Hinduism throughout the centuries. The term "yoga" is derived from the Sanskrit root "*yuj*," meaning to yoke or unite. The various yogic traditions, therefore, are seen as viable ways to attain liberation.

In keeping with the great appreciation for diversity within Hinduism, it is recognized that there is not just one, but four distinct paths (*margas*) to attaining enlightenment, each involving a different yogic practice:

Jnana Yoga (the Path of Self Knowledge) is based upon the ideas and practices described in the *Upanishads*. The most radical approach to Jnana Yoga is represented by the Advaita Vedanta, a non-dualistic tradition that emphasizes the oneness of Brahman and Atman. Through the use of practices like Self-Affirmation and Discrimination, an individual overcomes the ignorance (*advidya*) that keeps him estranged from his true nature and attains the liberation that comes from recognizing his true nature as Brahman.

A very different approach to liberation is represented by Bhakti Yoga (the Path of Devotion). Whereas the Jnana uses reason to attain liberation, the *bhakta* uses love and devotion towards a particular deity to achieve this end. The emphasis in this approach is on the cultivation of deep emotion or feeling, rather than on reason.

For those who are more actively inclined, Hinduism also offers Karma Yoga (The Path of Action). This is the path of selfless action and service towards others and was a path that Gandhi followed.

Finally, for the more mystically-inclined, Raja Yoga (The Path of Meditation) offers a scientific approach to mastering the mind through the practice of meditation.

In Hinduism it is believed that any of these four paths can lead one to liberation. The key is to find a yogic tradition that is best suited to the temperament, personality, and belief system of the individual. A more traditionally religious individual—particularly one who is emotionally inclined—would be advised, for example, to practice Bhakti Yoga, while a more philosophical type might be encouraged to practice Jnana Yoga. In Hinduism, it is believed that for every type of individual, there is a yogic path for which that person would be ideally suited.

The next step on the path to liberation would be to make a conscientious effort to follow this path as one's daily practice. As with any practice—learning to play an instrument, physical training, etc.—the benefits of the practice come only over time and to the extent that one works to incorporate the practice into one's daily life.

One final word of caution: the philosophical systems or worldviews underlying these traditions are often seen as mutually compatible in Hinduism. Metaphysically, however, one has to recognize that some of the yogic traditions are in fact conceptually incompatible. Yogic paths like Bhakti Yoga or Raja Yoga are dualistic, meaning that they recognize two realities in the universe—material and spiritual. A Yogic tradition like Jnana Yoga is strongly monistic. In this tradition, there is one true reality—Brahman—and everything in the universe, despite appearances to the contrary, is viewed simply as a manifestation of this one reality.

 Selection 2.6 — Why Four Different Paths?

NOTES

1. Jeaneane Fowler.. *Hinduism: Beliefs and Practices* (Brighton, GB: Sussex Academic Press, 1997): 7.
2. Julius Lipner. *The Hindus: Their Religious Beliefs and Practices* (New York: Routledge, 1998): 8

THE FOUR YOGAS

PERSONALITY TYPE	YOGA	PRACTICE	FOCUS ON	WORLDVIEW
PHILOSOPHICAL VISIONARY EXPANSIVE	JNANA YOGA (Yoga of Self-Knowledge) (aka VEDANTA)	DISCRIMINATION SELF-AFFIRMATION ("I am That")	Intellect	Monistic
EMOTIONAL PASSIONATE ROMANTIC RELIGIOUS	BHAKTI YOGA (Yoga of Devotion)	DEVOTIONAL (Chanting, Praying, Mantra)	Emotions	Dualistic
ACTIVE IN THE WORLD DOING CARING FOR OTHERS EXTROVERTIVE	KARMA YOGA (Yoga of Selfless Action)	SELFLESS ACTION	Body	Monistic or Dualistic
CONTEMPLATIVE MEDITATIVE INTROVERTIVE STILL CONCENTRATIVE	RAJA YOGA (The Yoga of Meditation) (aka ROYAL YOGA)	MEDITATION PRANAYAMA (Breathing)	(Psychic) Energy	Dualistic

3. *Bhagavad Gita* 2.20-25. Trans. Eknath Easwaran (Tomales, CA: Nilgiri Press, 2007): 90-91.
4. *Bhagavad Gita* 2.13, 89-90.
5. David Knipe. *Hinduism* (San Francisco: HarperCollins, 1991): 98.
6. Thomas Hopkins. *The Hindu Religious Tradition* (Belmont, CA: Wadsworth, 1971): 75.
7. *The Vedanta Sutra with the Commentary by Sankaracarya* 1.3.38. Trans. George Thibaut. *Sacred Books of the East*. Vol. 34 (1890): 228.
8. Nikhilananda, Swami. *Self-Knowledge (Atmabodha)* (New York: Ramakrishna-Vivekananda Center, 1980): 18.

SOURCES

 ## 2.1 — The Origins of the Self

Brihadaranyaka Upanishad

At that time the world was undifferentiated. It became differentiated by means of name and form, as the saying is: "He has such a name, such a form." Even today this world is differentiated just by name and form, as the saying is: "He has such a name, such a form."

He entered in here, even to the fingernail-tips, as a razor would be hidden in a razor-case, or fire in a fire-holder. People do not see him, for [as seen] he is incomplete. When one breathes, he becomes that breath (*prana*); when one speaks, voice; when one sees, the eye; when one hears, the ear; when one thinks, the mind: these are merely the names of his acts. Whoever worships one or another of these does not comprehend; for he is incomplete with one or another of these. Instead, one should worship with the thought that he is just one's Self (*Atman*), since in this way all these become one. That same thing—namely, this Self—is the trace of this All, for by it one knows this All—just as one might find by a footprint. Whoever knows this finds fame and praise.

Robert Ernest Hume, trans. Brihadaranyaka Upanishad 1.4.7 *The Thirteen Principle Upanishads*. London: Oxford University Press, 1921.

2.2 — Reincarnation

Brihadaranyaka Upanishad

The Soul at Death

35. As a heavily loaded cart goes creaking, just so this bodily self, mounted by the intelligent Self, goes groaning when one is breathing one's last.

36. When he comes to weakness whether he come to weakness through old age or through disease this person frees himself from these limbs just as a mango, or a fig, or a berry releases itself from its bond; and he hastens again, according to the entrance and place of origin, back to life.

37. As noblemen, policemen, chariot-drivers, village-heads wait with food, drink, and lodgings for a king who is coming, and cry: "Here he comes! Here he comes!" so indeed do all things wait for him who has this knowledge and cry: "Here is Brahma coming! Here is Brahma coming!"

38. As noblemen, policemen, chariot-drivers, village-heads gather around a king who is about to depart, just so do all the breaths gather around the soul at the end, when one is breathing one's last.

FOURTH BRAHMANA

1. When this self comes to weakness and to confusedness of mind, as it were, then the breaths gather around him. He takes to himself those particles of energy and descends into the heart. When the person in the eye turns away, back to the sun, then one becomes non-knowing of forms.

2. "He is becoming one," they say; "he does not see." "He is becoming one," they say; "he does not smell." "He is becoming one," they say; "he does not taste." "He is becoming one," they say; "he does not speak." "He is becoming one," they say; "he does not hear." "He is becoming one," they say; "he does not think." "He is becoming one," they say; "he does not touch." "He is becoming one," they say; "he does not know." The point of his heart becomes lighted up. By that light the Self departs, either by

---

Robert Ernest Hume, trans. Brihadaranyaka Upanishad. *The Thirteen Principle Upanishads.* London: Oxford University Press, 1921.

the eye, or by the head, or by other bodily parts. After him, as he goes out, the life goes out. After the life, as it goes out, all the breaths go out. He becomes one with intelligence. What has intelligence departs with him. His knowledge and his works and his former intelligence [i.e. instinct] lay hold of him.

The Soul of the Unreleased After Death

3. Now as a caterpillar, when it has come to the end of a blade of grass, in taking the next step draws itself together towards it, just so this soul, in taking the next step strikes down this body, dispels its ignorance and draws itself together for making the transition.

4. As a goldsmith, taking a piece of gold, reduces it to another newer and more beautiful form, just so this soul, striking down this body and dispelling its ignorance, makes for itself another newer and more beautiful form like that either of the fathers, or of the Gandharvas, or of the gods, or of Prajapati, or of Brahma, or of other beings.

5. Truly, this soul is Brahma, made of knowledge, of mind, of breath, of seeing, of hearing, of earth, of water, of wind, of space, of energy and of non-energy, of desire and of non-desire, of anger and of non-anger, of virtuousness and of non-virtuousness. It is made of everything. This is what is meant by the saying "made of this, made of that."

According as one acts, according as one conducts himself, so does he become. The doer of good becomes good. The doer of evil becomes evil. One becomes virtuous by virtuous action, bad by bad action.

But people say : "A person is made not of acts, but of desires only." In reply to this I say: As is his desire, such is his resolve; as is his resolve, such the action he performs, what action (karma) he performs, that he procures for himself.

 ## 2.3 — The Nature of Karma

The Law of Manu

Action [*karma*], which springs from the mind, from speech, and from the body, produces either good or evil results; by action are caused the various conditions of men, the highest, the middling, and the lowest.

Know that the mind is the instigator here below, even to that action which is connected with the body and which is of three kinds, has three locations, and falls under ten heads.

Types of Karmic Action

The three kinds of sinful mental action: (1) Coveting the property of others, (2) thinking in one's heart of what is undesirable, and (3) adherence to false doctrines.

The four kinds of evil verbal action: (4) Abusing others, (5) speaking untruth, (6) detracting from the merits of all men, and (7) talking idly.

The three kinds of wicked bodily action: (8) Taking what has not been given, (9) injuring creatures without the sanction of the law, and (10) holding criminal intercourse with another man's wife.

A man obtains the result of a good or evil mental act in his mind, that of a verbal act in his speech, that of a bodily act in his body.

In consequence of many sinful acts committed with his body, a man becomes in the next birth something inanimate; in consequence of sins committed by speech, a bird or a beast; and in consequence of mental sins he is reborn in a low caste.

That man is called a true tridandin in whose mind these three, (1) the control over his speech, (2) the control over his thoughts, and (3) the control over his body, are firmly fixed.

That man who keeps this threefold control over himself with respect to all created beings and wholly subdues desire and wrath thereby assuredly gains complete success.

If the soul chiefly practices virtue and vice to a small degree, it obtains bliss in heaven, clothed with those very elements.

The Law of Manu. Chapter 12. Trans. George Bühler. *Sacred Books of the East*. Vol. 25. Ed. Max Muller. Oxford: Oxford University Press, 1886. Translation updated.

But if it chiefly cleaves to vice and to virtue in a small degree, it suffers, deserted by the elements, the torments inflicted by Yama [the Lord of death].

The individual soul, having endured those torments of Yama, again enters, free from taint, those very five elements, each in due proportion.

Let man, having recognized even by means of his intellect these transitions of the individual soul, which depend on merit and demerit, always fix his heart on the acquisition of merit.

2.4 — Origins of Caste-Dharma

The Law of Manu

In order to protect this universe He, [Purusha] the most resplendent one, assigned separate (duties and) occupations to those who sprang from his mouth, arms, thighs, and feet.

To Brahmins (priests) he assigned teaching and studying (the Veda), sacrificing for their own benefit and for others, giving and accepting (of alms).

The Kshatriya (warriors) he commanded to protect the people, to bestow gifts, to offer sacrifices, to study (the Veda), and to abstain from attaching himself to sensual pleasures;

The Vaisya (merchants) to tend cattle, to bestow gifts, to offer sacrifices, to study (the Veda), to trade, to lend money, and to cultivate land.

One occupation only the lord prescribed to the Sudra (peasants), to serve meekly even these (other) three castes.

Man is stated to be purer above the navel (than below); hence the Self-existent One has declared the purest (part) of him (to be) his mouth.

As the Brahmin sprang from (Brahman's) mouth, as he was the first-born, and as he possesses the Veda, he is by right the lord of this whole creation.

For the Self-existent One, having performed austerities, produced him first from his own mouth, in order that the offerings might be conveyed to the gods and manes and that this universe might be preserved.

What created being can surpass him, through whose mouth the gods continually consume the offerings intended for them and the manes those intended for them?

Of created beings the most excellent are said to be those which are animated; of the animated, those which subsist by intelligence; of the intelligent, mankind; and of men, the Brahmins;

Of the Brahmins, those learned (in the Veda) are the best; of the learned, those who recognise (the necessity and the manner of performing the prescribed duties); of those who possess this knowledge, those who perform them; of the performers, those who realize the Brahman.

The very birth of a Brahmin is an eternal incarnation of the sacred law (*dharma*); for he is born to (fulfil) the sacred law, and becomes one with Brahman....

The Law of Manu. Trans. George Bühler. *Sacred Books of the East*. Vol. 25. Ed. Max Muller. Oxford: Oxford University Press, 1886. Translation updated.

 **2.5 — The Four Stages of Life**

The Law of Manu

CHAPTER II

The First Stage of Life: Studentship

Having performed the rite of initiation, the teacher must first instruct the pupil in the rules of personal purification, of conduct, of the fire-worship, and of the twilight devotions. But a student who is about to begin the Study of the Veda, shall receive instruction after he has sipped water in accordance with the Institutes of the sacred law, has made the Brahmanjali (proper salutation), has put on a clean dress, and has brought his organs under due control.

Let him always pronounce the syllable Om at the beginning and at the end of a lesson in the Veda; for unless the syllable Om precedes the lesson, it will slip away from him, and unless it follows it will fade away. Seated on blades of Kusa grass with their points to the east, purified by Pavitras (blades of Kusa grass), and sanctified by three suppressions of the breath (Pranayama), he is worthy to pronounce the syllable Om.

A wise man should strive to restrain his organs which run wild among alluring sensual objects, like a charioteer his horses....Through the attachment of his organs to sensual pleasure a man doubtlessly will incur guilt; but if he keep them under complete control, he will obtain success in gaining all his aims. Desire is never extinguished by the enjoyment of desired objects; it only grows stronger like a fire fed with clarified butter. If one man should obtain all those sensual enjoyments and another should renounce them all, the renunciation of all pleasure is far better than the attainment of them.

Those organs that are strongly attached to sensual pleasures cannot so effectually be restrained by abstinence from enjoyments as by a constant pursuit of true knowledge.

Neither the study of the Vedas, nor liberality, nor sacrifices, nor any self-imposed restraint, nor austerities, ever procure the attainment of rewards to a man whose heart is contaminated by sensuality.

That man may be considered to have really subdued his organs who, on

The Law of Manu. Trans. George Bühler. *Sacred Books of the East*. Vol. 25. Ed. Max Muller. Oxford: Oxford University Press, 1886. Translation updated.

hearing and touching and seeing, on tasting and smelling anything, neither rejoices nor repines.

But when one among all the organs slips away from control, thereby man's wisdom slips away from him, even as the water flows through the one open foot of a water-carrier's skin.

Let an Aryan who has been initiated daily offer fuel in the sacred fire, beg food, sleep on the ground, and do what is beneficial to this teacher, until he performs the ceremony of Samavartana on returning home.

An Aryan must study the whole Veda together with the Rahasyas [secret interpretations], performing at the same time various kinds of austerities and the vows prescribed by the rules of the Veda.

The student who has been initiated must be instructed in the performance of the vows and gradually learn the Veda, observing the prescribed rules.

But a student who resides with his teacher must observe the following restrictive rules, duly controlling all his organs, in order to increase his spiritual merit.

Every day, having bathed, and being purified, he must offer libations of water to the gods…, and place fuel on the sacred fire.

Let him abstain from honey, meat, perfumes, garlands, substances used for flavoring food, women, all substances turned acid, and from doing injury to living creatures. [Let him also abstain from] anointing his body, applying collyrium to his eyes, [and] from the use of shoes and of an umbrella or parasol, [and] from sensual desire, anger, covetousness, dancing, singing, and playing musical instruments, [and also from] gambling, idle disputes, backbiting, and lying, [and] from looking at and touching women, and from hurting others.

Let him always sleep alone, let him never waste his manhood; for he who voluntarily wastes his manhood, breaks his vow.

Let him not pronounce the mere name of his teacher without adding an honorific title behind his back even, and let him not mimic his gait, speech, and deportment.

By censuring his teacher, though justly, he will become in his next birth an ass, by falsely defaming him, a dog; he who lives on his teacher's substance, will become a worm, and he who is envious of his merit, a larger insect.

CHAPTER III

The Second Stage of Life: Householder

The vow of studying the three Vedas under a teacher must be kept for thirty-six years, or for half that time, or for a quarter, or until the student has perfectly learnt them.

A student who has studied in due order the three Vedas, or two, or even one only, without breaking the rules of studentship, shall enter the order of householders.

Having bathed, with the permission of his teacher, and performed according to the rule the Samavartana the rite on returning home, a twice-born man shall marry a wife of equal caste who is endowed with auspicious bodily marks [on the palms of the hands and on the soles of the feet].

For the first marriage of twice-born men, wives of equal caste are recommended; but for those who through desire proceed to marry again the following females, chosen according to the direct order of the castes, are most approved.

It is declared that a Shudra woman alone can be the wife of a Shudra, she and one of his own caste the wives of a Vaisya, those two and one of his own caste the wives of a Kshatriya, those three and one of his own caste the wives of a Brahmin.

A Shudra woman is not mentioned even in any ancient story as the first wife of a Brahmin or of a Kshatriya, though they lived in the greatest distress.

Twice-born men who, in their folly, wed wives of the low [*shudra*] caste, soon degrade their families and their children to the state of Shudras.

A Brahmin who takes a Shudra wife to his bed, will after death sink into hell; if he begets a child by her, he will lose the rank of a Brahmin.

The Position of Women

Women must be honored and adorned by their fathers, brothers, husbands, and brothers-in-law, who desire their own welfare.

Where women are honored, there the gods are pleased; but where they are not honored, no sacred rite yields rewards.

Where the female relations live in grief, the family soon wholly perishes; but that family where they are not unhappy ever prospers.

The houses on which female relations, not being duly honored, pronounce a curse, perish completely, as if destroyed by magic.

Hence men who seek their own welfare, should always honor women on holidays and festivals with gifts of ornaments, clothes, and dainty food.

In that family, where the husband is pleased with his wife and the wife with her husband, happiness will assuredly be lasting.

CHAPTER IV

The Brahmin Householder

Having dwelt with a teacher during the fourth part of a man's life, a Brahmin shall live during the second quarter of his existence in his house, after he has wedded a wife.

A Brahmin must seek a means of subsistence which either causes no, or at least little pain to others, and live by that except in times of distress.

For the purpose of gaining bare subsistence, let him accumulate property by following those irreproachable occupations which are prescribed for his caste, without unduly fatiguing his body.

Let him never, for the sake of subsistence, follow the ways of the world; let him live the pure, straightforward, honest life of a Brahmin.

He who desires happiness must strive after a perfectly contented disposition and control himself; for happiness has contentment for its root, the root of unhappiness is the contrary disposition.

Let him, untired, perform daily the rites prescribed for him in the Veda; for he who performs those according to his ability, attains to the highest state.

Whether he be rich or even in distress, let him not seek wealth through pursuits to which men cleave, nor by forbidden occupations, nor let him accept presents from any giver whosoever he may be.

Let him not, out of desire for enjoyments, attach himself to any sensual pleasures, and let him carefully obviate an excessive attachment to them by reflecting on their worthlessness in his heart.

Let him avoid all means of acquiring wealth which impede the study of the Veda; let him maintain himself anyhow, but study, because that devotion to the Veda-study secures the realization of his aims.

Let him walk here on earth, bringing his dress, speech, and thoughts to a conformity with his age, his occupation, his wealth, his sacred learning, and his race.

Let him never, if he is able to perform them, neglect the sacrifices to the sages, to the gods, to the Bhutas [cosmic spirits], to men, and to the manes....

Let him not dance, nor sing, nor play musical instruments, nor slap his limbs, nor grind his teeth, nor let him make uncouth noises, though he be in a passion.

Let him not give to a Shudra advice, nor the remnants of his meal, nor food offered to the gods; nor let him explain the sacred law to such a man, nor impose upon him a penance. For he who explains the sacred law to a Shudra or dictates to him a penance, will sink together with that man into the [dreadful] hell called Asamvrita.

Rules for all Householders

Let him, untired, follow the conduct of virtuous men, connected with his occupations, which has been fully declared in the revealed texts and in the sacred tradition (*smriti*) and is the root of the sacred law.

Through virtuous conduct he obtains long life, through virtuous conduct desirable offspring, through virtuous conduct imperishable wealth; virtuous conduct destroys the effect of inauspicious marks [on the palms of the hands and on the soles of the feet].

For a man of bad conduct is blamed among people, constantly suffers misfortunes, is afflicted with diseases, and shortlived.

A man who follows the conduct of the virtuous, has faith and is free from envy, lives a hundred years, though he be entirely destitute of auspicious marks.

Unrighteousness, practiced in this world, does not at once produce its fruit, like a cow; but, advancing slowly, it cuts off the roots of him who committed it.

If the punishment falls not on the offender himself, it falls on his sons; if not on the sons, at least on his grandsons; but an iniquity once committed never fails to produce fruit to him who wrought it.

He prospers for a while through unrighteousness; then he gains great good fortune; next he conquers his enemies; but at last he perishes branch and root.

Let him always delight in truthfulness, obedience to the sacred law, conduct worthy of an Aryan, and purity; let him chastise his pupils according to the sacred law; let him keep his speech, his arms, and his belly under control.

Giving no pain to any creature, let him slowly accumulate spiritual merit for the sake of acquiring a companion in the next world, just as the white ant gradually raises its hill.

For in the next world neither father, nor mother, nor wife, nor sons, nor relations stay to be his companions; spiritual merit alone remains with him.

Single is each being born; single it dies; single it enjoys the reward of its virtue; single it suffers the punishment of its sin....

CHAPTER VI

The Third Stage of Life: The Forest Dweller

A twice-born *snataka* (a Brahman who has completed his studentship), who has thus lived according to the law in the order of householders, may, taking a firm resolution and keeping his organs in subjection, dwell in the forest, duly observing the rules given below.

When a householder sees his skin wrinkled, and his hair white, and the sons of his sons, then he may resort to the forest.

Abandoning all food raised by cultivation and all his belongings, he may depart into the forest, either committing his wife to his sons, or accompanied by her.

Taking with him the sacred fire and the implements required for domestic sacrifices, he may go forth from the village into the forest and reside there, duly controlling his senses.

Let him offer those five great sacrifices according to the rule, with various kinds of pure food fit for ascetics, or with herbs, roots, and fruit.

Let him wear a skin or a tattered garment; let him bathe in the evening or in the morning; and let him always wear his hair in braids, the hair on his body, his beard, and his nails being unclipped.

Let him perform the Bali-offering with such food as he eats and give alms according to his ability; let him honor those who come to his hermitage with alms consisting of water, roots, and fruit.

Let him be always industrious in privately reciting the Veda; let him be patient of hardships, friendly towards all, of collected mind, ever liberal and never a receiver of gifts, and compassionate towards all living creatures.

Let him either roll about on the ground, or stand during the day on tiptoe, or let him alternately stand and sit down; going at the Savanas (at sunrise, at midday, and at sunset) to find water in the forest in order to bathe.

In summer let him expose himself to the heat of five fires, during the rainy season live under the open sky, and in winter be dressed in wet clothes, thus gradually increasing the rigor of his austerities.

When he bathes at the three Savanas (sunrise, midday, and sunset), let him offer libations of water to the manes and the gods and, practicing harsher and harsher austerities, let him dry up his bodily frame.

Having reposited the three sacred fires in himself, according to the prescribed rule, let him live without a fire, without a house, wholly silent, subsisting on roots and fruit.

Making no effort to procure things that give pleasure, chaste, sleeping on the bare ground, not caring for any shelter, dwelling at the roots of trees.

From Brahmins who live as ascetics, let him receive alms barely sufficient to support life, or from other householders of the twice-born castes who reside in the forest.

Or the hermit who dwells in the forest may bring food from a village, receiving it either in a hollow dish of leaves, in his naked hand, or in a broken earthen dish, and may eat eight mouthfuls.

These and other observances must a Brahmin who dwells in the forest diligently practice and, in order to attain complete union with the supreme Soul [Atman], he must study the various sacred texts contained in the Upanishads, as well as those rites and texts which have been practiced and studied by the sages (Rishis) and by Brahmin householders in order to increase their knowledge of Brahman, and also their austerity, and in order to sanctify their bodies.

Or let him walk, fully determined and going straight on, in a north-easterly direction, subsisting on water and air, until his body sinks to rest.

A Brahmin, having got rid of his body by one of those modes practiced by the great sages, is exalted in the world of Brahman, free from sorrow and fear.

The Fourth Stage of Life: The Wandering Ascetic (Sannyasin, Sadhu)

But having thus passed the third part of a man's natural term of life in the forest, he may live as an ascetic during the fourth part of his existence, after abandoning all attachments to worldly objects.

He who after passing from order to order, and after offering sacrifices and subduing his senses, becomes tired with giving alms and offerings of food, is an ascetic who gains bliss after death.

Having studied the Vedas in accordance with the rule, having begat sons according to the sacred law, and having offered sacrifices according to his ability, he may direct his mind to the attainment of final liberation.

A twice-born man who seeks final liberation without having studied the Vedas, without having begotten sons, and without having offered sacrifices, sinks downwards.

Having performed the Ishti, sacred to the Lord of creatures (Prajapati), where he gives all his property as the sacrificial fee, having reposited the sacred fires in himself, a Brahmin may depart from his house as an ascetic.

For that twice-born man, by whom not the smallest danger even is caused to created beings, there will be no danger from any quarter after he is freed from his body.

Departing from his house fully provided with the means of purification, let him wander about absolutely silent, caring nothing for enjoyments that may be offered to him.

Let him always wander alone, without any companion, in order to attain final liberation, fully understanding that the solitary man, who neither forsakes nor is forsaken, gains his end.

He shall neither possess a fire nor a dwelling; he may go to a village for his food, [but] he shall be indifferent to everything, firm of purpose, meditating and concentrating his mind on Brahman.

A piece of broken pottery instead of an alms-bowl, the roots of trees for a dwelling, coarse worn-out garments, life in solitude, and indifference towards everything—these are the marks of one who has attained liberation.

Let him not desire to die; let him not desire to live; let him wait for his appointed time as a servant waits for the payment of his wages.

Let him patiently bear hard words; let him not insult anybody; and let him not become anybody's enemy for the sake of this perishable body.

Against an angry man let him not in return show anger; let him bless when he is cursed; and let him not utter speech devoid of truth....

Delighting in what refers to the Soul [*Atman*], sitting in the postures prescribed by Yoga, independent of
external help, entirely abstaining from sensual enjoyments, with himself for his only companion, he shall live in this world, desiring the bliss of final liberation.

Let him seek to obtain alms without explaining prodigies and omens, without using his skill in astrology and palmistry, without giving advice, and without offering exposition of the Shastras.

Let him not in order to beg go near a house filled with hermits, Brahmins, birds, dogs, or other mendicants.

His hair, nails, and beard being clipped, carrying a broken pot, a staff, and a water-pot, let him continually wander about, controlling himself and not hurting any creature.

Let him go to beg once a day; let him not be eager to obtain a large quantity of alms. An ascetic who eagerly seeks alms attaches himself also to sensual enjoyments.

When no smoke ascends from the kitchen, when the pestle lies motionless, when the embers have been extinguished, when the people have finished their meal, when the remnants in the dishes have been removed, then let the ascetic go to beg.

Let him not be sorry when he obtains nothing nor rejoice when he obtains something; let him accept so much only as will sustain life; let him not care about the quality of his utensils.

By eating little, and by standing and sitting in solitude, let him restrain his senses, if they are attracted by sensual objects.

By the restraint of his senses, by the destruction of love and hatred, and by the abstention from injuring creatures, he becomes fit for immortality.

Let him reflect on the transmigrations of men, caused by their sinful deeds, on their falling into hell, and on the torments in the world of Yama [the God of Death]; on the separation from their dear ones, on their union with hated men, on their being overpowered by age and being tormented with diseases; on the departure of the individual soul from this body and its new birth in another womb, and on its wanderings through ten thousand millions of existences; on the infliction of pain on embodied spirits, which is caused by demerit, and the gain of eternal bliss, which is caused by the attainment of their highest aim, gained through spiritual merit.

By deep meditation let him recognize the subtle nature of the supreme Soul [*Atman*], and its presence in all organisms, both the highest and the lowest.

In order to preserve living creatures, let him always by day and by night, even with pain to his body, walk, carefully scanning the ground.

In order to expiate the death of those creatures which he unintentionally injures by day or by night, an ascetic shall bathe and perform six suppressions of his breath.

Let him recognize by the practice of meditation the progress of the individual soul through beings of various kinds, a progress hard to understand for unregenerate men.

He who possesses true insight into the nature of the world is not fettered by his deeds; but he who is destitute of that insight, is drawn into the circle of births and deaths.

By not injuring any creatures, by detaching the senses from objects of enjoyment, by the rites prescribed in the Veda, and by rigorously practicing austerities, men gain that state even in this world.

Let him quit this dwelling [his body], composed of the five elements, where the bones are the beams, which is held together by tendons instead of cords, where the flesh and the blood are the mortar, which is thatched with the skin, which is foul-smelling, filled with urine and ordor, infested by old age and sorrow, the seat of disease, harassed by pain, gloomy with passion, and perishable.

He who leaves this body, be it by necessity as a tree that is torn from the river-bank or freely like a bird that quits a tree, is freed from the misery of this world, which is dreadful like a shark.

Making over the merit of his own good actions to his friends and the guilt of his evil deeds to his enemies, he attains the eternal Brahman by the practice of meditation.

When by the disposition of his heart he becomes indifferent to all objects, he obtains eternal happiness both in this world and after death.

He who has in this manner gradually given up all attachments and is freed from all the pairs of opposites reposes in Brahman alone.

All that has been declared above depends on meditation; for he who is not proficient in the knowledge of that which refers to the Soul [*Atman*] reaps not the full reward of the performance of rites.

Let him constantly recite those texts of the Veda which refer to the sacrifice, those referring to the deities, and those which treat of the Soul [*Atman*] and are contained in the concluding portions of the Veda (*Vedanta*, *Upanishads*).

A twice-born man who becomes an ascetic after the successive performance of the above-mentioned acts shakes off sin here below and reaches the highest Brahman.

2.6 — Why Four Different Paths?

Swami Vivekananda

In people we see so many different natures. There are thousands and thousands of varieties of minds and inclinations. A thorough generalization of them is impossible, but for our practical purpose it is sufficient to have them characterized into four classes. First, there are the active people, the workers; they want to work, and there is tremendous energy in their muscles and their nerves. Their aim is to work—to do charitable deeds, build hospitals, make streets, plan and organize. Then there are the emotional people, who are able to love deeply the sublime and the beautiful. They love to think of the beautiful, to enjoy the aesthetic side of nature, and to adore Love and the God of Love. They love with their whole heart the great souls of all times, the prophets of religions, and the Incarnations of God on earth; they do not care about the exact date when the Sermon on the Mount was preached or the exact moment of Krishna's birth; what they care for is their personalities, their loveable figures. Such is their ideal. This is the nature of the lover, the emotional person. Then there is the mystic, whose mind wants to analyze its own self, to understand the workings of the human mind, what forces there are working inside, and how to know, manipulate, and obtain control over them. This is the mystical mind. Then there is the philosopher, who wants to weigh everything and use his or her intellect to experience even beyond the possibilities of all human philosophy.

Now a religion, in order to satisfy the largest proportion of humanity, must be able to supply food for all these various types of minds; and where this capability is wanting, the existing sects all become one-sided. Suppose you go to a sect that preaches love and emotion. They sing and weep, and preach love. But as soon as you say, "My friend, that is all right, but I want a little reason and philosophy; I want to understand things step-by-step and more rationally," they turn you away. That sect can only help people of an emotional turn of mind. They cannot provide what others need.

Again, there are philosophers who talk of the wisdom of India and the East using big psychological terms. But if a simple person goes to them and says, "Can you tell me anything to make me more spiritual, more loving?" the first thing they would do would be to smile and say, "Oh, first you need to be further along in your reason. What can you understand

Swami Vivekananda. *The Four Yogas*. New York: SophiaOmni, 2017.

about spirituality?" Once again, they are only able to help those who are inclined to their way. Then there are the mystical sects who speak all sorts of things about different planes of existence, different states of mind, what the power of the mind can do, and so on. But if you are an ordinary man and say, "Show me the good works that I can do; I am not much given to speculation. Can you give me anything that will suit my spiritual needs?" they will smile and say, "Poor man; he doesn't understand the way, he knows so little."

This is the existing condition of religion. What I want to propagate is a religion that will be equally acceptable to all minds; it must be equally philosophical, equally emotional, equally mystical, and equally conducive to action. If professors from colleges come, scientists and physicists, they will want reason. Let them have it as much as they want. Religion must be able to show them how to realize the philosophy that teaches us that this world is one, that there is but one existence in the universe. Similarly, if mystics come, we must welcome them, be ready to give them the science of mental analysis, and practically demonstrate it before them. If emotional people come, we must sit, laugh, weep, and "drink the cup of love" with them in the name of the Lord. And if energetic workers come, we must work with them with all the energy that we have. This combination will be the ideal of the nearest approach to a universal religion.

To become harmoniously balanced in all these four directions is my ideal of religion. And this religion is attained by what we, in India, call Yoga—union with God. To the worker, it is union between the individual and the whole of humanity; to the mystic, between the lower and higher Self; to the lover, union with the God of Love; and to the philosopher, it is the union of all Existence. This is what is meant by Yoga. *Yoga* is a Sanskrit term, and each of these four divisions of Yoga has a different Sanskrit name. The person who seeks after this kind of union is called a Yogi. The workers are called Karma Yogis. Those who seek union through love are called Bhakti Yogis. Those who seek it through mysticism are called Raja Yogis. And those who seek it through philosophy are called Jnana Yogis. So this word *Yogi* comprises them all.

These various Yogas must be carried out in constant practice; mere theories about them will not do any good. First we have to hear about them, and then we have to think about them. We have to reason the thoughts out, impress them on our minds, and then we have to meditate on them, realize them, until at last they become our whole lives. No longer will religion remain a bundle of ideas or theories, nor merely an intellectual assent; it will enter into our very being. By means of intellectual assent, we may subscribe to many foolish things today, and change our minds altogether tomorrow. But true religion never changes, for true religion is the realization of our divinity, not talk, nor doctrine, nor theories, however beautiful they may be. It is all being and becoming, not hearing or acknowledging; it is the whole soul becoming one with the Universal Soul. That is religion.

PRACTICES

Getting In Touch with the Breath

We've seen that in Sanskrit the words "Self" (*Atman*) and "breath" (*atma*) are closely connected. In Hinduism, as in many other religious traditions, it is through the breath that one is thought to come into contact with one's vital essence, life force (*prana*) or spirit. The first step in getting in touch with your breath is simply to begin paying attention to your breathing.

Try the following simple exercise:

1. Sit comfortably on a chair or cushion with your back straight but relaxed and your hands resting gently on your lap.
2. Close your mouth and begin to breathe naturally through your nose (If for some reason it's difficult to breathe through your nose, feel free to breathe through your mouth instead).
3. Notice the feeling of the air as it passes through the tip of your nose and into your lungs and out again. If you're like most people, you've probably never taken the time simply to observe the process of respiration from beginning to end. It's miraculous, isn't it? Without being able to breathe, we simply couldn't go on living, and yet we often take this vital bodily function totally for granted.
4. Now take a deep, deep, slow, slow breath, filling your lungs with oxygen. Hold the breath in your lungs for a few moments and just relax, allowing your body to settle down. Take a few seconds to appreciate the peacefulness and tranquility that comes from just being with the breath.
5. When the retention of the breath in your lungs begins to become uncomfortable, relax and slowly exhale. Allow the air to move naturally out of your lungs and your nostrils.

Now try the practice a few more times, slowly breathing in again, holding your breath, and allowing the breath to escape naturally from your body. Take note of any sensations or feelings that occur at each stage of this process—on the in-breath, at the retention of your breath, and on the out-breath.

Getting familiar with your breath may seem like a fairly simple practice, and it is! But this basic exercise, if developed, can have enormous physical, psychological, and spiritual benefits over time. If you don't believe me try doing deep, conscious breathing the next time you feel agitated, angry, or flustered. Imagine for example, that you're on line at the supermarket, picking up some food for dinner and the line is moving at an interminably slow pace. You're agitated because you're in a rush to get home and you can feel the anger and frustration building up inside of you. Instead of acting the way you typically would—obsessing over the injustice of the world or even exploding at the cashier—try doing some deep breathing instead. See for yourself if this practice helps calm you down in moments like this that are all too common in daily life.

What you actually are learning to do when you become better acquainted with your breath is also the foundation for the most basic form of meditation in Hinduism and in most of the major religious traditions of the world—breath meditation.

Beginning to Meditate: Turning Inward

As we've seen, a main conviction in Hinduism is that there is a Spiritual Self (*Atman*) that represents the authentic you. To get in touch with that spiritual element that lies at the core of your being, it's necessary to take time every now and then to turn away from the distractions of the external world and move the focus of your attention inward.

In ordinary life we tend to identify ourselves with the most obvious aspects of our human personality. As we move deeper and deeper inward, we see that none of these things can rightly be identified as the essence of who we are. Instead, through the practice of meditation, we come to realize that there is a dimension to our human identity...and this is your spiritual Self.

Many people think of meditation as something esoteric or a practice that involves special instructions from a teacher or guru. In fact, you were already beginning to meditate while you were getting acquainted with your breath in the previous exercise. Far from being a difficult practice suitable only for the spiritually advanced, basic meditation is something anyone can do: If you can breathe, you can meditate.

Here's the basic practice:

1. Sit comfortably on a chair or cushion with your back straight but relaxed and your hand resting gently on your lap. Close your eyes and allow your shoulders to drop naturally.
2. Begin with a positive intention—for example, this famous one

we've already encountered from the *Brhadaranyaka Upanishad* (1.3.28). To remind you that you are doing something spiritually important, place the palms of your hands together in front of your chest with your fingers pointing upwards as you say or chant these words (the classic "Namaste" or "peace" gesture):

> *Lead me from the unreal to the real.*
> *Lead me from darkness to light.*
> *Lead me from death to immortality.*

Your intention is to practice meditation for the sake of attaining liberation. When you say the words, say them as though you mean them and allow their import to penetrate your inner consciousness.

3. Now begin to breathe as you learned to do in the above exercise—slowly and deliberately. Observe the breath as it flows into your nostrils and begins to fill up your lungs. Don't think about breathing…experience the process of breathing and how the breath feels within your body. This is not an intellectual activity.

4. When you've taken as much oxygen in your lungs as is comfortable for you, hold it in your lungs for a few moments. Allow your body to settle down and become tranquil. If thoughts or emotions arise, just let them go…They're not important right now. Just rest peacefully in the quiet bliss of your own inner being.

5. When you feel the need, simply allow the air in your lungs to be released, flowing naturally out of your nostrils.

6. Continue to meditate for at least ten minutes. The more the better, but don't be obsessive about it.

7. As you begin to meditate on the breath, you'll notice that all sorts of things around you are potential sources of distraction—various bodily discomforts, the temperature in the room (either too hot or too cold), noises around you, etc. Just try to forget them and focus instead on your breath. Your aim is to begin to develop an internal life and to stop obsessing over trivial matters in the world around you. If you find yourself incapable of ignoring a distraction, take a few sharp, quick breaths to refocus your mind and then resume your deep breathing as usual.

8. End with the following affirmation from the *Taittiriya Upanishad* (1.1). Again, place the palms of your hands together in front of your chest with your fingers pointing upwards as you say or chant these words:

May the Lord of day grant us peace.
May the Lord of night grant us peace.
May the Lord of sight grant us peace.
May the Lord of might grant us peace.
May the Lord of speech grant us peace.
May the Lord of space grant us peace.
I bow down to Brahman, source of all power.
I will speak the truth and follow the law.
Guard me and my teacher against all harm.
Guard me and my teacher against all harm.
OM Shanti Shanti Shanti

3
JNANA YOGA

Jnana Yoga is the path of knowledge. The knowledge being referred to here is not ordinary knowledge but knowledge of the true nature of the Self (*Atman*). As Huston Smith defines it, *jnana* is "an intuitive discernment that transforms, turning the knower eventually into that which she knows."[1]

The approach taken to liberation in Jnana Yoga is actually quite different from the other yogic traditions. For one thing, the literature associated with this form of yoga tends to be quite abstract. This is a path, therefore, that is best suited for those with decidedly philosophical temperaments.

Jnana Yoga historically has been viewed as the most difficult of the four yogic paths—an approach that requires great powers of intellectual discrimination. In the Upanishads, this path is described as being "sharp as a razor's edge, impassable, and difficult to travel."[2] Since Hinduism recognizes multiple paths to attain liberation, most human beings in fact would be better off practicing one of the other yogic paths—Bhakti Yoga, Karma Yoga, or Raja Yoga.

Sources of Jnana Yoga

The original source of the teachings of Jnana Yoga can be found in that body of Hindu literature known as the *Upanishads,* a collection of religious texts that are part of the Vedas. There are over 200 surviving *Upanishads*, but about 13 of these are considered principle *Upanishads*.

The word Upanishad comes from *upa* (near) and *shad* (to sit), meaning "to sit down near." The image here is one of a disciple sitting down at the feet of a guru in order to receive spiritual instruction. Indeed most of the texts in the Upanishads involve some form of dialogue between a pupil and guru.

The *Upanishads* were written between 800 and 400 BCE, during a period in which some Indians were beginning to question the ritualistic emphasis placed on spiritual life that one finds in Vedic Religion and were looking for a more intensely personal spiritual practice. During this period, a spiritual shift occurred from emphasis placed upon external rites to an internal search for meaning, from formal sacrificial rituals to mystical insight into the nature of the Self.

Of course, we should not see the ideas contained in the Upanishads as being a total break from Vedic tradition, since they are part of the same *sruti* tradition. If there is a difference between the two, it is in approach— the *Upanishads* being more abstract and philosophical in nature than the texts that we find, for examine, in much of the *Rig Veda*. The texts also tend to be much more mystical in nature, calling the reader inward, rather than to the external world of rights and rituals.

In some of the Upanishads, however, there is a clear recognition that the kind of formalistic and formulaic rituals described in the Vedas could never lead one to liberation. For that a much deeper practice was needed— one that replaced empty ritualism with a more penetrative insight into the nature of reality itself.

 Selection 3.1 – From Ritual to Knowledge

It should be noted that the Upanishads represent the ideas of many different teachers and, therefore, do not represent a unified body of thought. The views contained in these texts, therefore, are varied and at times contradictory. If there is an essential idea running through these texts, it involves speculation about the relationship of Brahman and *Atman*—the Absolute and the Self. The most profound of the Upanishads, as we shall see, posit a relationship that is far more intimate than anything one finds in earlier Vedic texts.

Various strands of Jnana Yoga can also be found in the Hindu system of thought know as Vedanta—one of the six orthodox schools of Hindu philosophy. The term "Vedanta" literally means "the end of the Vedas" or the "fulfillment of the Vedas." Originally this term applied specifically to the Upanishads, which were literally the last part of the Vedas, but by the early 5th century BCE Vedanta emerged as its own philosophical system for interpreting these texts.

Like the Upanishads themselves, Vedanta is concerned with the relationship between Brahman and *Atman*. Even within this school, however, various, and at times conflicting, approaches to this relationship were proposed, ranging from complete non-dualism or monism (*Advaita Vedanta*) to qualified non-dualism (*Vishishtadvaita Vedanta*) to complete dualism

(*Dvaita Vedanta*).

The oldest, most influential, and original of these approaches is that of *Advaita Vedanta*, particularly as represented by the radical non-dualistic teachings of the 8th century philosopher Adi Shankara. In surviving works such as *Crest-Jewel of Discrimination* and *A Thousand Teachings*, Shankara presents a radical and profound affirmation of the oneness of all reality that would eventually become a dominant influence on the rest of Indian philosophy.

Brahman: The Absolute

As we've seen, traditional Hinduism is dualistic in its understanding of reality. In dualistic forms of Hinduism, two dimensions of realities are recognized: Pure Spirit (*Purusha*) and matter (*prakriti*). This can also be described in terms of the dichotomy between body and spirit, God and nature. The approach of the Jnana Yoga, by comparison, is monistic: There is only one reality in the universe and this is Brahman—the Supreme Being. Brahman alone is real in the sense of being changeless and eternal.

In Hindu thought, Brahman can be understood in two ways. *Saguna Brahman* is God with attributes (wisdom, power, goodness, etc.). This approach to talking about Brahman uses what is known in Western philosophy as the *via positive* (the positive way to talk about God). *Nirguna Brahman* is God without attributes. Because any attributes we ascribe to the Divine are necessarily limiting, during the time of the Upanishads there was the recognition that human beings could only describe Brahman in negative terms. For example, in the *Mundaka Upanishad*, Brahman is described in the following way:

> That which is invisible, ungraspable, without source, without color,
> Without sight or hearing, without hand or foot
> Eternal and all-pervading, omnipresent, extremely subtle—
> That is the Imperishable, which the wise understand to be the source
>   of all being.[3]

This method of attempting to discover what Brahman is like, by focusing on what he is not, is the *via negative* (the negative way). As Jeaneane Fowler writes, "it is important to realize that Brahman is not negative *nothingness*, but a no-thingness and therefore cannot be subject to the kinds of statements which can be made about things in the cosmos."[4]

Typically, when one refers to Brahman in this second sense, the term that is often used is The Absolute or Ultimate Reality, since such terms are abstract enough to prevent one from falling into the trap of assigning specific attributes to God. Occasionally, you'll hear Brahman referred to in Vedantic literature as *"Satchitananda"* (*sat* = pure being; *chit* = pure consciousness; *ananda* = pure bliss). This designation is considered acceptable because it talks about Brahman as source of all reality, conscious thought, and ultimate happiness, while not necessarily imposing any limitations.

In essence Brahman is the total and absolute reality in the universe. As we read in the *Mundaka Upanishad*:

Brahman truly is immortal.
Brahman before, Brahman behind,
Brahman to the right and to the left, stretched forth below and above.
Brahman, truly, is nothing other than this whole universe.[5]

If Brahman is one, eternal, and changeless and if all things are manifestations of Brahman, then it follows that all reality, therefore, is one and changeless. This is not some particular deity who one worships in some sacrificial right. Brahman is the totality of all that is.

 Selection 3.2 — Brahman as Totality

The Identity of Atman and Brahman

If everything in the universe is one with Brahman, then it follows that we are one with Brahman as well. Or to put it even more radically, our true essence—*Atman*—is Brahman.

The famous formula that is used to express this identity is found in the sixth chapter of *Chandogya Upanishad*: *"Tat Tvam Asi."* In this text, Svetaketu returns home from his life as a student of the Vedas. His father asks him whether during the course of his studies, he had learned about the nature of the Self. When he laments that he hasn't, his father provides him with a series of analogies to describe the true nature of the Self, each of which ends with the refrain, *"Tat Tvam Asi."* This literally means "that you are." Svetaketu—indeed all human beings—are nothing other than the Self, Brahman, the Absolute.

If our natures are identical to Brahman's, then our nature is also *Satchitananda*. We are Pure Being, Pure Consciouness, and Pure Bliss. Liberation in Jnana Yoga comes from this insight into our true nature. As we read in the *Brihadaranyaka Upanishad*, "Whoever knows 'I am Brahman' becomes this All."[6]

Selection 3.3 — The Nature of the Self

Maya

The basic problem that many people have with a monistic approach to reality is that it doesn't seem to make sense. In our everyday life, we perceive multiplicity and change. So how do we account for such multiplicity? The answer is that our impressions of multiplicity and change are due to the illusionary power of *maya* (illusion). The term suggests that reality as we perceive it is not necessarily as it actually is. Or to put it more colloquially, "Things ain't what they seem to be." *Maya* gives the impression that the world of multiplicity and change are real, when in fact the world that we perceive is illusionary or unreal—at least in comparison to Brahman. As we read in the *Svetasvatara Upanishad*, "This whole world, the illusion-maker (*mayin*) projects out of this reality. And in it by illusion (*maya*) the other (individual soul) is confirmed."[7]

To help illustrate the Hindu concept of *maya*, we can use the example of a dream state. When we're dreaming, things in our dreams seem real to us. We know, however, that they're not when we are awake. Jnana yoga makes the following analogy: Our ordinary way of experiencing the world is similar to a dream state. The world of matter and change may seem real to us, but those who have a higher state of consciousness recognize the world of multiplicity and change to be illusionary.

The Cause of Bondage

Bondage and suffering in Jnana are seen as due to the Self identifying with the body or mind out of ignorance (*avidya*). Through ignorance we have forgotten our true natures and instead erroneously believed ourselves to be small, limited individuals.

But ignorance is simply the absence of knowledge. An analogy that is used frequently in Jnana Yoga is of a person stumbling in darkness who grabs onto a piece of rope and mistakenly believes it to be a snake. The person's ignorance can only be removed by shedding light (i.e., knowledge) upon it.

Swami Vivekananda uses the famous parable of the lion who thought he was a lamb to make a similar point:

> There is a story about a lioness who was big with child. Going about in search of prey, and seeing a flock of sheep, she jumped upon them. She died in the effort, and a little baby lion was born,

motherless. He was taken care of by the sheep, and they brought him up. He grew up with them, ate grass, and bleated like the sheep. And although in time he became a big, full-grown lion, he still thought he was a sheep. One day, another lion came in search of prey and was astonished to find that in the midst of this flock of sheep was a lion, fleeing like the sheep at the approach of danger. He tried to get near the sheep-lion to tell him that he was not a sheep but a lion, but the poor animal fled at his approach. However, he watched his opportunity, and one day found the sheep-lion sleeping. He approached him and said, "You are a lion!" "I am a sheep," cried the other lion; he could not believe the contrary, but bleated. The lion dragged him to a lake and said, "Look here; there is my reflection and there is yours." Then came the comparison. The sheep-lion looked at the lion and then at his own reflection, and in a moment came the idea that he was a lion. The lion roared; the bleating was gone.[8]

The point that Vivekananda is making in the parable is that we are lions who think of ourselves as lambs. We ignorantly think of ourselves as finite, imperfect beings when in fact we are infinite and perfect. It is only when we truly know our authentic natures (the lion cub seeing his reflection in the water) that we can begin to live in an authentic way (roaring instead of bleating like a lamb).

Liberation in Jnana Yoga

The path to liberation in Jnana Yoga cannot be through acts of devotion towards a personal God, since such devotion only serves to increase the illusion of duality (e.g., making a distinction between the devotee and the object of devotion). It also serves to limit Brahman by assigning positive attributes to what is essentially beyond all attribution. So any practices emphasizing worship, sacrifice, or prayer are clearly problematic in Jnana Yoga.

Instead, liberation in Jnana Yoga comes through the attainment of the right knowledge (*vidya*) of the identity of *Atman* and Brahman—the profound realization, in other words, that "I am Brahman." It involves recognizing reality as it is, not as it appears to the mind clouded by ignorance.

If the individual self is not real, then it also follows that bondage and liberation are also unreal. Both ideas are also the result of ignorance. If there is no one bound, then, of course, there is no one to be liberated. Any chains that we have upon us are therefore self-imposed.

Abandoning the world of duality, the Jnana Yogi archives the highest state of Self-Awareness: everything in the universe is perceived as one and all duality is transcended. "By realizing the Self as Brahman," writes Swami Adiswarananda, "the aspirant sees Brahman everywhere; everything outside becomes nothing more than a reflection of everything inside" with the result that "all perceptions of diversity are overpowered by an awareness of all-pervasive unity."[9] This state is described in the Upanishads in the following way: "As flowing rivers disappear in the sea, losing their names and forms, so a wise man, freed from name and form, attains [Brahman], who is greater than Great. He who knows the Supreme Brahman, truly becomes Brahman."[10]

The Practice of Jnana Yoga

Two basic practices are emphasized in Jnana Yoga—discrimination and self-affirmation.

The practice of discrimination aims at deepening the mind's consciousness of Self by rejecting everything that is not Self. It begins by asking the question, "Who am I?" In answering this question, it is important to note that in Jnana Yoga, *Atman* is not the same as the individual self or finite personality (*jiva*) that is subject to the effects of karma and rebirth. This individual self is enclosed within five sheaths (*kosas*) or material layers that are like the layers of an onion. These sheaths include the physical body, the vital force, the mind, the intellect, and bliss. These obscure our true natures, and therefore we need to get beyond our identification with these elements.

In Jnana Yoga this means answering the question, "Who am I?" by first becoming aware of what I am not. Thus in the *Birhadaranyaka Upanishad* we read that the Self "is that which has been described as *neti, neti* (not this, not that). It is imperceptible, for It is not perceived; undecaying, for It never decays; unattached, for It is never attached; unfettered, for It never feels pain and never suffers injury."[11]

The Jnani begins by asking the question, "What am I?" He then explores each of the five sheaths, asking "Is this the Self?" And he answers "*neti, neti*" recognizing that all these attributes are limiting and therefore can't be who we really are. In the end, we are left with "I am," pure awareness—in other words, with the Self alone.

The second common practice used in Jnana Yoga is that of Self-Affirmation. This is nothing other than the continual practice of affirming our true natures as *Atman*/Brahman. A wonderful example of this practice is found in the the *Ashtavakra Gita* (The Song of Ashtavakra), a text in the Vedanta tradition which deals with the nature of the Self, Brahman, and liberation through knowledge. In this text, King Janaka asks the sage

Ashtavakra how he can attain liberation. Ashtavakra replies that he is to train himself to recognize who he truly is, and to him Janaka replies with a mantra that affirms his identity with Brahman: "O I am spotless, tranquil, pure consciousness and beyond nature."

If one wants to attain liberation, however, it's not simply enough just to keep repeating Self-affirming mantras like this one. You need to be open enough to allow the truth of the mantra to penetrate your consciousness. To quote a famous like from the same text, "As you think, so shall you become."

 Selection 3.4 — Discrimination & Self-Affirmation

NOTES

1. Huston Smith. *The World's Religions* (San Francisco: Harper-Collins, 1961): 29.
2. *Katha Upanishad* 1.3.14. Unless otherwise noted, all translations from the Upanishads in the text are the Editor's.
3. *Mundaka Upanishad* 1.1.6.
4. Jeaneane Fowler. Hinduism: Beliefs and Practices (Brighton, GB: Sussex Academic Press, 1997): 114.
5. *Mundaka Upanishad* 1.2.11.
6. *Brihadaranyaka Upanishad* 1.4.10.
7. *Svatasvtara Upanishad* 4.9.
8. Swami Vivekananda. "The Real Nature of Man." Delivered at the Royal Institute of Painters in Watercolors, London, June 21, 1896.
9. Swami Adiswarananda. *The Four Yogas* (Woodstock, VT: Skylight Paths): 242.
10. *Mundaka Upanishad* 3.2.8-9.
11. *Brhadaranyaka Upanishad* 4.4.22.

SOURCES

 ## 3.1 — From Ritual to Knowledge

The Unsteady Vessels of Rites
[Mundaka Upanishad]

This is the truth.

The sacrificial rites that the sages saw in the sacred hymns were described in many ways in the three Vedas. Perform them diligently, you lovers of the truth, for that is your path that leads to the world of good works. When the flames of the sacrificial fire begin to flicker, then place your offerings made in faith on that fire....

But these boats of sacrifice are unsteady vessels. Unsteady are the eighteen books which explain these lower ceremonial rites. The unwise who praise these rites fall victim again and again to old age and death. Dwelling in ignorance but believing themselves wise and learned, these fools stagger about aimlessly, like the blind leading the blind.

As they wander along the path of ignorance, like children they think to themselves, "We have accomplished our aim!" These performers of rituals do not realize the truth because of their desires, and thus they fall into misery when the rewards of their actions have been exhausted. Considering sacrifices and good works as the best, these foolish ones do not know of any higher good. They receive a heavenly reward for their efforts, but then are forced to reenter this world or even a lower one.

But those who practice austerity and faith, dwelling in peace in the forest, wise and freed from passions, pass through the door of the son to the immortal, imperishable Self.

Having discerned the worlds won by works, let the seeker renounce them. The world that was not made cannot be won by what is made (i.e., sacrifices). For that knowledge, let him go forth...to a teacher (*guru*) who is filled with wisdom and well-established in the realization of Brahman. To the seeker who has approached his teacher, whose thoughts are untroubled by desires, who has attained perfect peace, should the teacher impart the knowledge of Brahman, whereby one knows the eternal and the true.

Mundaka Upanishad 1.2.1-2; 7-13. Trans. A.J. Grunthaler.

# 3.2 — Brahman as Totality

That Alone is Brahman
[Kena Upanishad]

The student asks:

What is it that makes the mind think?
What is it that gives the body its first breath?
What compels us to utter these words?
What is that Spirit that directs the eyes and ears?

The teacher replies:

It is the ear of the ear, the eye of the eye, the word of the word, the mind of the mind, and the life of the life. Passing beyond the senses, the wise, on departing from this world, become immortal.

There the eye cannot go, nor speech, nor mind. We do not know, we do not understand, how one would teach it. It is above both the known and the unknown—so we have heard from the ancients who have explained this.

That which is not uttered by words, but by which words are uttered—that alone is known as Brahman, and not what people worship here.

That which is not thought by the mind, but by which the mind thinks—that alone is known as Brahman, and not what people worship here.

That which is not seen by the eye, but by which the eye sees—that alone is known as Brahman, and not what people worship here.

That which is not heard by the ear, but by which the ear hears—that alone is known as Brahman, and not what people worship here.

That which is not breathed, but by which the breath is breathed—that alone is known as Brahman, and not what people worship here.

Kena Upanishad 1.1-8. Trans. A.J. Grunthaler.

3.2 — The Nature of the Self

In the Temple of the City of Brahman
[Chandogya Upanishad]

In the center of the city of Brahman (the body) is a small temple in the form of a lotus flow (the heart). And within that temple can be found a very small space. We should search out what dwells within that space and should desire to understand it.

If a student should ask, "Who dwells in the small temple in the form of a lotus flower in the center of the city of Brahman? What is it in there that should be sought after and what is there that one should desire to understand?"

Then the teacher should answer, "That little space in the heart is as vast as the entire universe. Within that space are contained heaven and earth, fire and wind, sun and moon, lightening and stars, all that of this world and all that is not."

If the student should ask, "If everything that exists is contained in that city of Brahman—all beings and all desires—then what remains of it when old age overcomes it or when it perishes?"

Then the teacher should answer, "That does not age when the body ages; That does not die when the body dies. This is the real city of Brahman. In it all desires are contained. That is the Self (*Atman*). It is free from old age, free from death, free from suffering, free from hunger and thirst. That Self is the fulfillment of all desires, the ultimate truth....

"Just as here on earth whatever is acquired through work perishes, so too whatever is acquired for the next world through good works perishes. Those who depart from this life without having realized the Self and what they truly desire—for them there is no true fulfillment here or in all the worlds. But those who depart from this life having realized the Self and what they truly desire—for them there is true fulfillment here and in all worlds....

"The Self is a bridge, a boundary for keeping these worlds apart. Neither day nor night can cross that bridge, nor old age, nor death, nor sorrow, nor good, nor evil. All evil is turned back from it, for evil cannot cross that bridge. That is why, when this bridge has been crossed, the blind are no longer blind, the sick no longer sick. And upon crossing that bridge the

---

Chandogya Upanishad 8.1.1-7; 4.1-3; 7.1. Trans. A.J. Grunthaler

night turns to day, for there is no darkness there...."

"The Self is beyond all sin, beyond decay and death, beyond hunger and thirst, beyond all sorrow; it desires nothing that is not good. It is That which one should seek out and understand. He who has found out and understands the Self obtains all worlds and fulfills all desires."

"You Are That"
[Chandogya Upanishad]

Om! There lived a boy named Svetaketu Aruni. One day his father said to him, "Svetaketu, go live the life of a student of sacred knowledge. There is no one in our family who hasn't studied the sacred Vedas and remains a Brahmin by family connections alone."

Having become a pupil by the age of twelve and having studied all the Vedas, Svetaketu returned home at the age of twenty-four, conceited and very proud of his abilities. His father said to him, "Svetaketu, since you are now so conceited and presume yourself learned, did you think to ask for that teaching whereby the not-heard has become heard, the not-thought has become thought, and the not-comprehended has become comprehended?"

"What is that teaching, father?" asked Svetaketu.

"My son, just as by knowing one lump of clay, all that is made of clay can become known, since any difference that arises is merely a matter of speech, while the clay alone is reality. And just as by knowing one piece of gold, all that is made from gold can become known, since any difference that arises is merely a matter of speech, while gold alone is the reality. And just as by knowing any individual thing made of iron, all that is made of iron can become known, since any difference that arises is merely a matter of speech, while the iron alone is reality."

"Surely those venerable teachers of mine did not know this," said Svetaketu, "For if they had known this, why would they not have mentioned this to me? Please sir, tell it to me."

"So be it," said his father.

"These rivers, my son, flow eastward towards the east and westward towards the west. They go from ocean to ocean. Merging, they become the ocean itself. And those rivers when they merge with the ocean do not know that they are this or that river.

"In the same way, my son, all these creatures, though they have come

---

Chandogya Upanishad 6.1, 10, 12, 13. Trans. A.J. Grunthaler.

forth from Being, do not know that they have come forth from Being. Whatever a creature may be here—whether a lion, or a wolf, or a boar, or a worm, or a fly, or a gnat, or a mosquito—that they become.

"That Being is the subtle essence that is the source of this great universe. That is Reality. That is the Self. You are That, Svetaketu."

"Please give me further instruction, father."

"So be it, my son," he replied.

"Bring me a fruit from that banyan tree."

"Here it is, sir."

"Break it."

"It is broken, sir."

"What do you see there?"

"These extremely small seeds, sir."

"Break one of them."

"It is broken, sir."

"What do you see there?"

"Nothing at all, sir."

Then his father said to Svetaketu, "That subtle essence which you do not perceive there—from that very essence comes this great banyan tree. Believe me, my son, a subtle essence is the source of this great universe. That is Reality. That is the Self. You are That, Svetaketu."

"Please give me further instruction, father."

"So be it, my son," he replied.

"Place this salt in water and then come see me in the morning."

Svetaketu did as he was told. His father said to him, "My son, bring me the salt which you placed in the water last night." Svetaketu looked for it, but could not find it, for of course it was completely dissolved.

"Take a sip of water from the side," said his father. "How is it?"

"It is salt."

"Take a sip from the middle," he said. "How is it?"

"It is salt."

"Take a sip from that end," he said. "How is it?"

"It is salt."

"Throw it away and come to me," his father said.

Svetaketu did as he was told, saying, "That salt, though unperceived, was there all the time."

Then his father said to Svetaketu, "In the same way, you do not perceive Being here; but it is indeed here. Believe me, my son, a subtle essence is the source of this great universe. That is Reality. That is the Self. You are That, Svetaketu...."

3.4 — Discrimination and Self-Affirmation

Six Stanzas on Nirvana
Adi Shankara

I am not the mind, the intellect, the ego, or the memory;
I am not the sense of sight, hearing, smell, taste, or touch;
I am not the earth, the air, the fire, the water, or the ether;
I am perfect knowledge and bliss—
I am That (Shiva)! I am That (Shiva)!

I am neither the energy nor the five vital forces;
I am neither the seven elements of the body nor the five sheaths;
I am not an organ of action like the mouth, the hands, the feet, or the
    tongue.
I am perfect knowledge and bliss—
I am That! I am That!

I have neither attachment nor aversion, neither greed nor delusion;
I have neither egotism nor pride, neither *dharma* nor *moksha*;
I have neither desires of the mind nor objects of desire.
I am perfect knowledge and bliss—
I am That! I am That!

I know nothing of either virtue or vice, nothing of pleasure or pain;
I have no need of mantras, sacred temples, scriptures, or sacrifices;
I am not the enjoyer, the enjoyed, or the act of enjoyment.
I am perfect knowledge and bliss—
I am That! I am That!

I have no death nor fear of death;
I have no caste, no father, no mother;
I have no friend, no family, no disciple, no guru.
I am perfect knowledge and bliss—
I am That! I am That!
I am without form, changeless, and all-encompassing.

Adi Shankara. "Six Stanzas on Nirvana." Trans. A.J. Grunthaler

I exist everywhere, with no attachments to this world;
I am unfathomable, beyond salvation.
I am perfect knowledge and bliss—
I am That! I am That!

Ashtavakra Gita

I

Janaka said:

[1] How is knowledge acquired? How is liberation attained? How can one achieve detachment? Please tell me this, sir?

Ashtavakra said:

[2] If you wish to attain liberation, my son, avoid the way of the senses like poison and seek out the nectar of patience, compassion, simplicity, and truthfulness.

[3] You are not earth, air, fire, water, or ether. If you wish to attain liberation, recognize you are the Self—pure consciousness, the witness of all of these.

[4] Detach yourself from the body and rest in pure consciousness. Then you will attain peace, fulfillment, and freedom from bondage.

[5] You don't belong to any caste or to any stage of life. You are beyond sight, beyond form, the witness of all things. Therefore be happy.

[6] Right and wrong, pleasure and pain—these are of the mind, not of you. You are neither the doer nor the enjoyer of actions. You are completely free.

[7] You are the witness of all things, and forever free. The sole source of your bondage is that you see yourself as something other than this.

[8] Bitten by the black snake of egotism, you think, "I am the doer." But if you drink the nectar of conviction and think, "I am not the doer," then you will become happy.

[9] Know you are the one pure consciousness. In the fire of this conviction the forest of ignorance shall be burnt down, freeing you from grief and restoring you to happiness.

―――――――

Ashtavakra Gita, Chs 1-2. Trans. A.J. Grunthaler.

[10] Just as a rope falsely seen appears to be a snake, so too is this universe of appearance misperceived. But you are supreme joy and consciousness, so be happy.

[11] If you think yourself free, then you are free; if you think yourself bound, then you are bound. Thus the saying is true, "As one thinks, so shall one become."

[12] The Self is the witness, all-pervading, one, perfect, completely free, unattached. It is desireless, and peaceful. Only through illusion does it seem to be part of the world of change (*samsara*).

[13] Meditate on your Self as the highest principle of consciousness, undivided. In doing so you will free yourself from the delusion of yourself as a separately existing entity.

[14] Because you have been trapped for so long in the delusion of the body as your true self, you have become bound. Cut through this delusion with the knowledge that you are pure awareness and be happy.

[15] In reality you are already unattached and actionless, luminous and pure. You are bound because you keep striving for altered states of consciousness (*samadhi*) [that are unnecessary].

[16] You pervade this universe and everything is made up of you. Your nature is pure consciousness. Stop being so small-minded!

[17] You are unconditioned, formless, immovable, unencumbered, unfathomable, and pure intelligence. Cling to consciousness alone.

[18] Simply realize that which has form is unreal and only the formless is real. Only when you comprehend the truth of this teaching will you escape from the possibility of further rebirth.

[19] Just as a mirror both reflects and stands apart from what it reflects, so too does the Highest Reality exist in the body and beyond it as well.

[20] Just as the same all-pervading space exists both within a pot and outside, so too does the all-encompassing Brahman exist everywhere and in all things.

II

Janaka said:

[1] Truly I am spotless and serene, pure consciousness and beyond nature. All this time I have been afflicted by delusion.

[2] Even as this body is given light by me, so too do I give light to everything in the universe. Therefore either this entire universe is mine, or else nothing at all.

[3] Having left behind this universe and this body, through wisdom I now

see my supreme Self.

[4] As waves, foam, and bubbles are still nothing other than water, so too are all the things that arise by the Self in this universe nothing other than the Self....

[7] It is only through ignorance of Self that the universe appears, but through knowledge of the Self it no longer appears. It is like the rope that appears to be a snake when wrongly seen; when the rope is seen for what it is, the snake disappears.

[8] My true nature is light and nothing other than that. When anything shines forth in the universe, it is only my light that is shining forth....

[9] This universe that appears in me is just an illusion due to ignorance, just as silver seems to appear in mother of pearl, the snake in the piece of rope, or the mirage of water in sunlight.

[10] Everything in the universe emanates from me and will eventually dissolve back into me, like the clay pot eventually returns to the earth, waves into water and a bracelet melted back into gold.

[11] Oh, how wonderful I am, how glorious! For me there is no end, and I will survive even as the entire universe, from Brahma down to the smallest tuft of grass, is swept away.

[12] Oh, how wonderful I am, how glorious! Though immersed in form, I am still one. I neither come nor go anywhere, but am present everywhere and in all things....

[14] Oh, how wonderful I am, how glorious! I possess nothing at all and at the same time everything that can be thought or spoken of.

[15] The knower, the act of knowing, and the known—these do not exist in reality. I am the stainless Self out of which these three appear due to ignorance.

[16] Dualism is the cause of suffering. The only cure for this is the recognition that all is experienced is unreal and that I am the one stainless consciousness....

[18] For me there is no bondage or freedom. All this illusion has disappeared. Truly, this universe exists only in me, although in reality it does not exist in me at all....

[20] This body, heaven and hell, bondage and liberation, and fear—all these are simply products of the imagination. What have these things to do with me, whose nature is pure consciousness?

[22] I am not this body, nor is this body mine; I am not a separate entity. I am pure consciousness itself. I am bound only because of my thirst for life.

[23] I am the infinite ocean upon which the differentiated waves of the universe are produced out of the winds arising from the mind.

[24] In that same infinite ocean, the winds of thought are stilled, and the

world of this individual self is brought to an end.

[25] How wonderful it is that I am the infinite ocean in which the waves of individual beings naturally arise, collide with one another, play for a time, and then disappear.

PRACTICES

CHANTING OM/AUM

OM (or AUM) is considered the primordial sound, the sacred vibration and perfect expression of that ultimate reality that is Brahman. As we read in the *Mandukya Upanishad*:

> OM! This syllable is all that is....
> It is everything in the past, the present, and the future.
> It is that which is beyond space, time, and causality (1.1).

Chanting this sound has been known to bring peace to body and mind by merging the vibrations of the body with that of the universe (It is said that the sound Om, when chanted, vibrates at the frequency of 432 Hz, which is the same vibrational frequency found throughout everything in nature). For spiritual people, the sound is also considered the divine sound and chanting it gets one in touch with the divine reality within oneself.

Here's how you do the AUM chant:

- Take a deep in-breath. You should feel the oxygen rising through your body from the navel—the very core of your body.
- On the out-breath chant AUM as if it were three elongated syllables:
  o The "A" is elongated and pronounced like "aaaaaa" with the mouth wide open.
  o The "U" is elongated and pronounced like "oooo" with the mouth tightening into a circle.
  o The "M" is elongated and pronounced like "mmmm" with the lips now together and your teeth gently touching.
  o End the out-breath with a moment of silence and stillness.
- Keep repeating this on the in- and out-breaths.

As you chant these syllables you should experience the sound starting in the back of your throat and chest with the "aaaaawe", moving into your throat with the "ooo", and ending with the sound of the "mmmm" vibrating through your head. The moment of silence and stillness at the end of the chant represents the perfect peace of the Absolute Being that you yourself are. Relish in this at the end of each out-breath.

Try this for about ten minutes and see how you feel.

CHANTING SOHAM

The word Soham comes from *Isha Upanishad* 16 and is based upon two Sanskrit words: "Sah" ("He" or "That") and "Ahem" ("I am"; "I exist"). The term then literally means, "I am he (or That)." It is said that when a child is born, it cries "Koham" ("Who am I?") and the universe cries back, "Sohum" (basically, "You are the same as I am."). The Soham mantra has been called the universal mantra because it is said to be connected with the breathing process, something common to all living things: Sooo is the sound of inhalation and Hummm is the sound of exhalation.

In using Soham as a mantra, you simply repeat the two syllables in your mind on the in- and out-breaths:

- Soooo is repeated in the mind with the in-breath.
- Hummmmm is repeated in the mind with the out-breath.

Soham can also be chanted in the following way:

- On the in-breath, slowly chant, "Sooooooo".
- On the out-breath, slowly chant, "Hummmmm."

Chant like this for about 10 minutes. As you chant this mantra try to feel in the very depths of your consciousness that you are in fact one with the Absolute Being that is the source of all things.

MANTRAS FOR SELF-AFFIRMATION

Mantras play an important role in Jnana Yoga and are used to affirm the identity of the Self with Brahman. The following statements from the Upanishads are called the *mahavkyas*—the great sentences—and are frequently used as mantras in this tradition:

Tat Tvam Asi ("You are That") [tat t'vam ass-i]
(*Chandogya Upanishad* 6.8.7)

Aham Brahmasmi ("I am Divine") [a-ham bra-mas-mi]
(*Birhadaranyaka Upanishad* 1.4.10)

Ayam Atma Brahma or just **Atma Brahma** ("This Self is Divine")
[a-yam at-ma brah-ma]
(*Mandukya Upanishad* 1.2)

Sarvam Khalvidam Brahma (Truly All is God)
[sar-vam kal-vi-dam brah-ma]
(*Chandogya Upanishad* 3.14.1)

Instructions

1. Choose one of the above mantras that resonates with you. Make sure that you repeat this mantra a few times to get the pronunciation right and to memorize it.
2. Make a commitment to sit with your mantra first thing in the morning to set the tone for your entire day. It's also beneficial to sit again with your mantra later on in the day (after work or school, before dinner, or before bed). Try to work with your mantra for at least 10 minutes each time you sit
3. Begin your mantra meditation by closing your eyes and breathing in deeply to relax your body and mind.
4. Become aware of the physical sensations in your body, your thoughts, and your feelings. Realize that "you are not these." These are merely manifestations of your more limited self (your *jiva*), but they can't possibly capture the majesty of what you truly are at the very core of your being. You are much more than your body, your mind, or your emotions, and more than the sum total of these.
5. After a minute or two begin to recite the manta in your mind over and over. Don't worry about trying to maintain a particular rhythm. Just allow the mantra to flow through your mind the way it wants to and without trying to force it in any way. You don't even need to think about the meaning of the mantra or whether you are pronouncing it correctly. Let go of such petty concerns. This should be a gentle and easy practice.
6. If thoughts enter you mind and you get distracted by them, just gently return to your mantra.
7. After about 15-20 minutes, just sit in silence for a minute or two, enveloped in stillness.

That's all there is to it!

After you're finished see how you feel: Do you feel more peaceful than you were before? Do you sense a blissful stillness inside you? Do you feel more positively about who you are at the deepest level of your being? If you answer yes to any of these questions, that's great. If not, try not to get frustrated. There are definitely benefits to this sort of meditation, but it might take a bit of consistent practice before these benefits begin to manifest themselves.

If after a few sessions of practice, you still have trouble with this practice, try chanting the mantra out loud several times before repeating it mentally. For some, chanting helps to concentrate the mind, making it easier for the internal repetition of the mantra to take hold.

4
BHAKTI YOGA

Hindu thought continued to develop during in the centuries after the composition of the Vedas. We've seen that there are two different classifications for Hindu literature: *sruti* and *smriti*. *Sruti* (revealed) literature includes the Vedas and the Upanishads and is considered the most sacred. This literature developed over many centuries as part of oral tradition and therefore cannot be assigned to any particular author or authors. *Smirti* (remembrance) literature by contrast was generally written down, and although it may have been revised over time, it is generally attributed to specific authors.

These *smirti* texts frequently make use of mythology and stories to convey higher truths and place an emphasis on devotional practice (*bhakti*) as the optimal path for the vast majority of human beings to attain liberation. Although recognition of the importance of a devotional attitude is present in the Vedas, it was around the first century BCE that this tendency in Hinduism became much more pronounced, with movements springing up devoted specifically to gods like Rama, Krishna, and Shiva.

Three important works were produced during this period, which are vital to understanding the development of Hindu thought, particularly as it pertains to Hindu devotionalism:

- *The Mahabharata* (400 BCE): This Indian epic describes the struggle between two branches of the same family—the Kauravas and the Pandavas. One of the most influential parts of the *Mahabharata* is the *Bhagavad Gita* ("The Song of the Lord"), which stands out as one of the most important spiritual texts ever written.
- *The Ramayana* (200-100 BCE): Another famous Indian epic, the *Ramayana*, tells the story of Rama—the seventh avatar of the god Vishnu—whose wife Sita is abducted by Ravana, the King of Lan-

ka (modern day Sri Lanka).

- *The Puruanas* (300-800 CE): The word "purana" means "ancient" or "old." There are18 major Puranas, the earliest of which is thought to have been composed during the third century CE.

Any one of these works, each of which is massive in length, could be the subject of a lifetime of study. Likewise, the specific ways that the practice of *bhakti* manifests itself could vary widely, depending upon the particular sect to which the devotee belonged. For our purposes, however, we can identify certain specific characteristics of all devotion—characteristics which apply not only to Hinduism but to almost every devotional form of religion.

What is Bhakti?

The term *bhakti* simply means "devotion." Bhakti Yoga, therefore, is the path of devotion. In fact, the vast majority of Hindus today practice *bhakti*. This is a spiritual path that is much more popular than Jnana, Karma, or Raja yoga because it is accessible to people of all ages, castes, and backgrounds.

The word "*bhakti*" comes from the Sanskrit *bhaj* meaning "to be attached to" or "to belong to." The goal of *bhakti*, in other words, is to unite the *bhakta* (devotee) with the Divine. This union, however, is not desired out of any selfish motives—for example, out of fear or the desire for reward here or in the next life—but for its own sake, or rather for the sake of the object of devotion.

Bhakti also involves intense feelings of love, passion, and yearning for the object of one's devotion. All real devotion by its very nature is an intensely emotional (i.e., non-intellectual) experience. In practice, bhakti is ecstatic in expression—manifesting itself in singing, dancing, and rapturous praise. This is definitely not a path for aloof intellectual types.

The ultimate goal of bhakti is self-surrender to the object of one's devotion. The parallels to romantic love are illustrative: the lover says to the beloved, "I'm yours complete, totally, without reservation" and means it. The lover surrenders his own goals and desires for the sake of the beloved. Something similar to this happens in spiritual devotion: the devotee surrenders will and ego for the sake of the object of devotion.

 Selection 4.1 — What is Devotion?

Knowledge and Devotion

Although both Jnana Yoga and Bhakti Yoga can lead to liberation, there are some significant differences between these two approaches. First, whereas Jnana Yoga is the path for an intellectual elite, Bhakti Yoga is the path for the many. This is the common approach to religion and spirituality that one finds practiced among ordinary adherents, not just in Hinduism, but in all the world's major religions. Most ordinary human beings are not coldly rational types, but fairly emotional. Thus, while a strong intellect is needed to practice Jnana Yoga, all that is required for Bhakti Yoga is an open, loving heart.

Second, we've seen that Jnana Yoga is totally monistic in worldview. In this approach nothing is ultimately real except God and the Self, which are seen as one. Bhakti Yoga, on the other hand, is contentedly dualistic. The *bhakta* sees himself as distinct from the God who is his ultimate love object.

Third, whereas Jnana Yoga seeks the eradication of the ego, Bhakti Yoga seeks its transformation and elevation. While the distance between God and the devotee is eradicated, the distinction between them never is. As Swami Adiswaranda puts it, "Its watchword is 'I am His' as distinguished from 'I am He.'"[1]

Finally, while the *jnana* relies totally on his own powers of discernment to achieve liberation, the *bhakta*, recognizing the limitations of his own abilities, seeks divine grace for liberation:

> Liberation is a gift of God. It cannot be acquired through austerity, penance, or meditation. Liberation is the redeeming grace of God who responds to our sincere prayers and who is sensitive to our needs, ever desirous of our love. God's grace is a heralding light that dispels the darkness of ignorance in our hearts and sets us free. Such grace is unconditional, spontaneous, and ever redeeming. The darkness of ignorance that had accumulated for thousands of years becomes dispelled as soon as the light of God's grace shines upon it.[2]

As in Christianity, a debate arose in Hinduism concerning the degree to which human effort was required for human liberation, with some schools arguing that God's grace must be met with effort on the part of the devotee and other schools arguing that all that is required for liberation is God's grace. But it's clear that in devotional Hinduism, as in Christianity, ultimate union with God cannot be achieved without at least some sort of divine assistance.

While it is often claimed that Jnana Yoga is compatible with Bhakti

Yoga, in fact these two forms of yoga are separated by vastly different worldviews, methods, and aims, and each path has its advocates. We saw that in the Upanishads, ritual devotion is viewed as a lower path than that of Self-knowledge. In *Bhagavad Gita*, on the other hand, while the path of knowledge is praised, the path of devotion is clearly viewed as the optimal one for most human beings. As Krishna proclaims:

> Those who set their hearts on me and worship me with unfailing devotion and faith are more established in yoga [than those who follow the path of knowledge]. As for those who seek the transcendent Reality, without name, without form, contemplating the Unmanifested, beyond the reach of thought and feeling, with their senses subdued and mind serene and striving for the good of all beings, they too will verily come to me. Yet hazardous and slow is the path to the Unrevealed, difficult for physical creatures to tread.[3]

Elsewhere in the text, Krishna describes one who is most perfectly established in yoga as he "who worships me in perfect faith, completely absorbed in me."[4] By the time of the *Bhagavad Gita*, then, the practice of devotion, far from being seen as an inferior path as it sometimes was viewed in the Upanishads, becomes the most direct way to achieve liberation.

This tension between the often divergent aims and practices of jnana and bhakti would be a prevailing one in Hindu thought. Although modern Vedantists such as the 19th century mystic Ramakrishna and his disciple Vivekananda made a valiant attempt to reconcile these two paths, the results are often philosophically problematic.

 Selection 4.2 – Knowledge and Devotion

Ishta-Deva as Object of Devotion

As we saw in the previous chapter, there are two ways that God is understood in Hindu thought. The first is God in his impersonal aspect—as transcendent, completely other, as the Absolute (Brahman). The problem with God in his impersonal aspect is that he is completely unreliable. How do you connect with the Absolute? How can you worship a being who is completely other than anything within your realm of experience?

Therefore, the devotee instead focuses on God in his personal aspect. In Bhakti Yoga there is the belief that the Absolute manifests itself on the level of creation, taking the form of some *avatar* (from the Sanskrit word "*avatara*", which means "descent") or incarnation of the divine. This kind of anthropomorphic tendency—the attribution of human characteristics or behavior to the divine—is present in almost every religion. What this does in practice is help make God more relatable to us and gives us a concrete object for our devotion.

In Christianity, Christ is recognized as the sole incarnation of God. In Hinduism, on the other hand, Brahman is believed to manifest himself in a multitude of different forms. It's said that there are 33 million deities in Hinduism. In fact, most educated Hindus recognize that there is only one God, but also believe that he can take many different forms on the level of creation. He reveals himself to peoples throughout history based upon their particular needs and circumstances.

The devotee in Bhakti Yoga is encouraged to find his or her own *Ishta-deva*. The term literally means "chosen," "cherished" or "preferred" deity and refers to one's own ideal form of the divinity. This represents the specific form of God that best suits the devotee's personality and temperament:

> The chosen Ideal of an aspirant may be any form of God....According to bhakti-yoga, the most natural object of love is a human form of God. We can best love God in a human way by establishing a human relationship with God. Bhakti-yoga advocates worship of the Chosen Ideal through concrete images and symbols that are reminiscent of the Chosen Ideal.[5]

By far the most significant deity worshipped by Hindus is Vishnu and his earthly avatars or incarnations. Although Vishnu was not an important deity in Vedic times, worship of him grew in India as that of Indra and Agni began to decline. Vishnu, as we saw in Chapter 2, is part of the Hindu trinity that includes Brahma (the Creator) and Shiva (the Destroyer). Vishnu's role is that of sustainer of the universe.

Hindus recognize ten incarnations (*dashavatara*) of Vishnu—nine which have already manifested themselves and one yet to occur. Included in these incarnations are mythical and historic figures such as Rama, Krishna, and the Buddha. It is said that the tenth and final incarnation of Vishnu in the form of Kalki ("Destroyer of Filth") will occur at the end of the Kali Yuga, our present age. At time he will appear atop a white horse, carrying a blazing sword and will usher in the end of time.

Of all the avatars of Vishnu, the most popular undoubtedly is Krishna, devotion to whom began in Northwestern India around the third century BCE. The rise of Krishna worship was partly due to the influence of the *Bhagavad Gita* ("Song of the Lord"), the impact of which on Hindu thought cannot be overstated. Many contemporary commentators have referred to the *Bhagavad Gita* as the "Hindu New Testament" with Krishna occupying a similar role as Jesus as savior of mankind. Describing his own role as *avatara* in Chapter Four of the Gita, Krishna says:

> My true being is unborn and changeless. I am the Lord who dwells in every creature. Through the power of my own [material nature] I manifest myself in a finite form.
>
> Whenever [righteousness] declines and the purpose of life is forgotten, I manifest myself on earth. I am born in every age to protect the good, to destroy evil, and to reestablish [righteousness].[6]

The Bhagavad Gita is the preeminent work of Hindu devotionalism. Although the text attempts a synthesis of all four yogic paths, it's clear that devotion to Krishna is considered to be the most direct and universal path to liberation. We'll have much more to say about the role of Krishna in the *Bhagavad Gita* in Chapter 7.

The Importance of the Guru

The *Ishta-deva* is often chosen for the devotee by his guru. In English, the term guru has come to connotate someone who is an expert or master in any field—for example a "tennis guru." The term has a more specific meaning in Hinduism. The syllable *gu* means "darkness" and the syllable *ru* means "dispeller." The guru is therefore literally one who dispels the darkness of ignorance from his student through his careful guidance and instruction. According to Joel Mlecko, "the guru is teacher, counselor, father-image, mature ideal, hero, source of strength, even divinity integrated into one personality." In devotional Hinduism, the guru, therefore, is indispensable for spiritual development.[7]

Gurus existed in Vedic times. They were typically Brahmins who trained students in Vedic recitation. In the Upanishads, the role of the Guru was to teach students knowledge of the Self. As you may recall from the previous chapter, the word "upanishad" itself refers to the act of sitting near a guru to have the esoteric wisdom of ultimate reality imparted.

With the rise of devotional Hinduism during the first few centuries of the Common Era, the role of the guru in Hindu thought began to evolve. Spiritual liberation in all the traditions of Hinduism is not something that can be attained completely on one's own. In the Bhakti tradition it was believed necessary to find someone to serve as a guide—ideally someone who had already attained liberation him- or herself—to serve as an example and to impart spiritual knowledge to the student. The guru in this tradition, therefore, is first and foremost a "teacher of the truth" (*sad-guru*)—the truth about reality, the truth about God, and the truth about the right path to realize God.

The student in turn was expected to honor the guru as his own parent and to serve his guru faithfully:

> There is not the least doubt that Guru is father, Guru is mother, and the Guru is God even; and, as such, he should be served by all with their thought, word, and deed.[8]

As this passage notes, the guru is also viewed as an embodiment of the Divine—a manifestation of God himself in human form and therefore deserving of the highest devotion himself.

Since the guru is so central in devotional Hinduism, an important question is how one goes about finding a proper guru. This is definitely not simply an academic question: classical Hindu texts suggest that even in ancient times, there were plenty of men posing as gurus, but who so lacked proper training that they would often lead students astray. Likewise, there was probably no shortage of scam artists who pretended to be reputable gurus, but who were more interested in taking advantage of prospective students. (That trend unfortunately continues today.) So first and foremost, the guru should be someone who has the highest knowledge of the spiritual wisdom and practices that he seeks to teach. Equally important, the teacher should be a person of great moral character—both to set the right moral example to the student, but also so that he isn't likely to abuse his position.

 Selection 4.3 — The Guru and the Student

The Practice of Bhakti Yoga: The Nine Forms of Devotion

Composed between the 8th and 10th centuries CE, the *Bhagavata Purana* is one of the most famous texts of devotional Hinduism. The text promotes devotion to the God Vishnu in the incarnation of Krishna and describes nine limbs or forms of devotion that a *bhakta* is encouraged to practice. You'll notice that the devotional practices recommended in the *Bhagavata Purana* are actually quite common to just about any devotional form of religion. These are practices that any devout Christian, Jew, or Muslim would probably find quite familiar.

These nine forms of devotion—ascending in intensity from lowest to highest, from the most superficial sort of practice to the most profound—include the following:

1. Listening (*shravana)* to the scriptures or stories concerning the deity.
2. Singing (*kirtana)* devotional songs (*kirtan*) in praise of the deity.
3. Remembering (*smarana*) the presence of the deity constantly by repeating his name (*japa*) in the form of a mantra.
4. Rendering service to others (*padasevana*) by combining the practice of selfless action (Karma Yoga) with devotion (Bhakti Yoga).
5. Worshipping (*archana*) the deity through rituals.
6. Prostration (*vedana*) before the image of the deity.
7. Developing the feeling of being the servant (*dasya*) of the divinity.
8. Developing the feeling of friendship (*sakhya*) with the divinity.
9. Self-offering (*atma-nivedana*)—the complete surrender of the self to the divinity (body, mind, and soul).

In keeping with the tolerant spirit of Hinduism, a devotee is encouraged to practice whichever form of devotion suits him or her best. It is believed that by engaging in any of the practices, a devotee remains constantly in the presence of God.

 Selection 4.4 — Worshipping the Lord

Bondage and Liberation in Bhakti Yoga

Bondage in Bhakti Yoga comes from egoistic desire. This is described in Bhakti Yoga as the fixation on "I and mine." Liberation conversely comes when we overcome our egoism by turning our minds and will to the divine rather than ourselves. It is a state in which "the feeling of 'I and mine' transforms into that of 'thou and thine.'"[9]

Liberation ultimately involves an attitude of surrender to God. Through complete and totally surrender the *bhakta* experiences union with God. "Fill your mind with me;" Krishna instructs Arjuna in the *Bhagavad Gita*, "love, me; serve me; worship me always. Seeking me in your heart, you will at least be united with me."[10]

Unlike in Jnana Yoga, this union doesn't eradicate the difference between human and divine:

The jnana experiences jada samadhi, in which no trace of "I" is left.
The samadhi attained through the path of bhakti is called "chetana

samadhi." In this samadhi there remains consciousness of "I"—the "I" of the servant-and-Master relationship, of the lover-and-Beloved relationship....God is the Master; the devotee is the servant. God is the Beloved; the devotee is the lover...."I don't want to be sugar. I want to eat it."[11]

The climax of intense devotional practice in Bhakti Yoga is mystical union with God—spiritually entering into the mystery of the divine. This experience is described in remarkably similar terms to the experiences of mystics in the Christian, Jewish, or Islamic traditions. Although mystical experiences are often said to be ineffable—in other words, they are unable to be fully comprehended by anyone who has not personally experienced them—an attempt is typically made to describe them using metaphorical language.

Mystical union with the divine in all these traditions is experienced by the devotee as ecstasy and rapture. It is often described by using the language of inebriation in which the devotee is drunk on the bliss of God or by using the even more highly charged language of sexual climax.

One of the most famous examples of this attempt to describe the ineffable in Hindu literature is found in the eleventh chapter of the *Bhagavad Gita*, in which Krishna reveals his cosmic form to his devotee Arjuna, who is awe-struck by the revelation. When Krishna returns to his human form, he explains to Arjuna:

> Neither knowledge of the Vedas, nor austerity, nor charity, nor sacrifice can bring the vision you have seen. But through unfailing devotion...you can know me, see me, and attain union with me. Those... who devote themselves to me completely...enter into me.[12]

At the end of the text, Krishna assures Arjuna that ultimate union with him is inevitable for those who are diligent in their devotion. "Be aware of me always," he said, "adore me, make every act an offering to me, and you shall come to me; for you are dear to me."[13] Here we have none of the intellectual hurdles of Jnana Yoga, the rigor associated with Karma Yoga, or the psychological complexities of Raja Yoga. In each of these other paths there is always the danger that the inability to master the specific practices of the yogic tradition could potentially thwart liberation. In the devotional texts of Bhakti Yoga, on the other hand, we have a virtual guarantee of spiritual success as long as one has faith and practices with sincerity.

 Selection 4.5 — Mystical Ecstasy

NOTES

1. Adiswarananda, Swami. *The Four Yogas* (Woodstock, VT: Skylight Paths, 2006): 84-85.
2. Adiswarananda, 90.
3. *The Bhagavad Gita* 12.2-5. Trans. Eknath Easwaran (Tomales, CA: Nilgiri Press, 2007): 207.
4. *The Bhagavad Gita* 6.47, 145.
5. Adiswarananda, 104.
6. *The Bhagavad Gita* 4.6-8, 117.
7. Mlecko, Joel D. *The Guru in Hindu Tradition.* Numen 29 (July 1982): 33.
8. *The Shiva Samhita.* Trans. Rai Bahadur Srisa Chandra Vasu (Bahadurganj, India: Bhuvaneswari Asrama, 1914): 25.
9. Adiswarananda, 91.
10. *The Bhagavad Gita* 9.34, 177.
11. Ramakrishna, *The Gospel of Ramakrishna* (Abridged Edition). Trans. Swami Nikhilananda (New York: Ramakrishna-Vivekananda Center, 1958): 311-312.
12. *The Bhagavad Gita* 11.53-55, 202.
13. *The Bhagavad Gita* 18.65, 264.

SOURCES

 ## 4.1 — What is Devotion?

Narada Bhakti Sutras

The Narada Bhakti Sutras are one of the most important works of Hindu devotional philosophy. Supposedly composed by the sage, Narada, we know little about the author of the text or when it was written. Like most Hindu instructional texts, the brevity of the aphorisms (sutras) contained in within it were intentional to help facilitate memorization by students.

The Definition and Benefits of Bhakti

[1] Now we shall explain the doctrine of devotion.

[2] Devotion is the highest and purest love for God.

[3] This pure love for God is eternal.

[4] Having obtained it, a person becomes perfect, immortal, and supremely satisfied.

[5] On gaining this, a person wants nothing, grieves over nothing, hates nothing, delights in nothing, and does not become enthusiastic over material pursuits.

[6] Experiencing this, a person becomes completely intoxicated, becomes overcome with ecstasy, and delights in the Self.

The Importance of Renunciation

[7] This love of the divine involves no element of (sensual gratification), because its essence is renunciation.

[8] Such renunciation (in the practice of devotional services) means abandoning all social conventions and religious rituals governed by Vedic injunctions.

[9] "Renunciation" also means exclusive devotion to the Lord and indifference to all things that are obstacles to this devotion.

[10] "Exclusive devotion" means giving up all other supports other than the Lord Himself.

Narada Bhakti Sutra 1-33. Trans. A.J. Grunthaler.

[11] "Indifference to things that are obstacles to devotion" means accepting only those social conventions and Vedic injunctions that are favorable to this devotional service.

[12] Even after steadfastness of conviction has been acquired, one should still strive to follow scriptural injunctions.

[13] Otherwise there is the possibility of falling away from the spiritual path.

[14] Therefore, as long as the body lasts one should continue to be engaged in normal social activities, such as the taking of food.

Descriptions of Bhakti

[15] Various descriptions of devotion are now given, corresponding to different authoritative options on the subject.

[16] Vyasa…claims that devotion is love of worship of the Lord in various ways.

[17] Garga states that devotion is love of sacred stories about Lord and so forth.

[18] Shandilya says that devotion is that which does not conflict with completion of the true Self.

[19] But Narada says that true devotion involves dedicating all one's acts to the Supreme Lord and the feeling of extreme distress in forgetting him.

[20] Devotion, in fact, is correctly described in each of these ways.

[21] A perfect illustration of devotion is found in the love of the cow-herding women of Vraja.*

[22] Even in the case of these women, they cannot be criticized for forgetting the glory of the Lord.

[23] On the other hand, those who forget the Lord's glory are no better than adulterers.

[24] In such false devotion, there is no idea of one being happy in the happiness of the other (ie., the Lord).

Bhakti as the Highest Goal of Life

[25] Pure devotion is superior to the path of action (Karma Yoga), the path

---

* These women were considered the ultimate example of bhakti, since they sacrificed everything (pleasure, family, reputation) in service of their devotion to Krishna. This devotion was questioned by some thinkers because it seemed as though their love was for the person of Krishna rather than for his divine being. This criticism is flatly rejected by Narada.

of Self-knowledge (Bhakti Yoga), and the path of mystic meditation (Raja Yoga).

[26] This is so because love is the foundation of the fruit of all these other paths.

[27] It is also superior because the Lord hates egotism and loves [the devotee's] humility.

[28] There are those who maintain that knowledge alone is the means to develop this love.

[29] Others consider devotion and knowledge mutually interdependent.

[30] But Narada, the son of Brahma, says that devotion is its own fruit.

[31] This fact is illustrated by the examples of a palace, a meal, and the like.

[32] A king would not be satisfied by mere knowledge of a palace or a meal.

[33] Therefore devotion to the Lord alone should be chosen by those seeking liberation.

4.2 — Knowledge and Devotion

Sri Ramakrishna

Sri Ramakrishna (1836-1886) was a 19th century Indian mystic, who was influenced by both the Bhakti and Vedanta traditions. The principle source of our information about the teachings of Ramakrishna comes from Mahendranath Gupta's The Gospel of Sri Ramakrishna, which presents an account of the last years of Ramakrishna's life from 1882-1886. The Gospel offers a vision of self-realization that combines Jnani and Bhakti yogic elements, although the emphasis in this work is clearly devotional.

The [*jnani*], who seeks to realize the Absolute Brahman, discriminates, saying: "Not this, not that." That is, the Absolute is not this, not that, not any finite object, not the individual soul, not the external world. When, as the result of this kind of reasoning, the heart ceases to be moved by desires; when, in fact, the mind is merged in superconsciousness, then [knowledge of Brahman] is reached. One who has truly attained to this [knowledge of Brahman] realizes that Brahman the Absolute alone is real, and the world is unreal, and that all names and forms are like dreams. What Brahman is cannot be described by word of mouth nor can one even say that He is personal. Such is the point of view of a non-dualist [*jnani*].

The dualistic devotees and lovers of the Personal God (*bhaktas*), on the contrary, accept all states as real. Unlike the non-dualists, they look upon the waking state as a reality and they do not hold that the external world is like a dream. They say that the external world is the glory of the Lord. The heavens, stars, moon, mountains, ocean, men, birds and beasts, all these He has created. He manifests His glory by these. He is both within and without. He dwells in our hearts. The most advanced *bhaktas* say that the Lord Himself manifests as the twenty-four [cosmic principles], that He appears as the individual soul and the external world. A *bhakta* wishes to enjoy communion with his Lord and not to become one with Him. His desire is not to become sugar, but to taste of it.

Do you know what are the innermost thoughts and feelings of a true devotee? He says: "O Lord! You are the Master, I am your servant. You are my Mother, and I am your child"…The dualistic devotee does not wish to

---

The Gospel of Ramakrishna. Trans. Swami Abhedananda. New York: Vedanta Society, 1907. Translation updated.

say, "I am Brahman...." (pp. 147-148)

People dispute among themselves, saying: "God is personal, with form. He cannot be impersonal and formless"... When realization comes, then all these questions are settled. He who has seen God can tell exactly what He is like. As Kavira said: "God with form is my Mother, God without form is my Father. Whom shall I blame, whom shall I praise? The balance is even." He is with form, yet He is formless. He is personal, yet He is impersonal, and who can say what other aspects He may have!

Four blind men went to see an elephant. One touched a leg of the elephant and said: "The elephant is like a pillar." The second touched the trunk and said: "The elephant is like a thick club." The third touched the belly and said: "The elephant is like a huge jar." The fourth touched the ears and said: "The elephant is like a big winnowing-basket." Then they began to dispute among themselves as to the figure of the elephant. A passer-by, seeing them thus quarrelling, asked them what it was about. They told him everything and begged him to settle the dispute. The man replied: "None of you has seen the elephant. The elephant is not like a pillar, its legs are like pillars. It is not like a big water-jar, its belly is like a water-jar. It is not like a winnowing-basket, its ears are like winnowing-baskets. It is not like a stout club, its trunk is like a club. The elephant is like the combination of all these." In the same manner do those sectarians quarrel who have seen only one aspect of the Deity. He alone who has seen God in all His aspects can settle all disputes.

Again: Two persons were hotly disputing as to the color of a chameleon. One said: "The chameleon on that palm-tree is of a red color." The other, contradicting him, replied: "You are mistaken, the chameleon is not red but blue." Not being able to settle the matter by argument, both went to the person who always lived under that tree and had watched the chameleon in all its phases of color. One of them asked him: "Sir, is not the chameleon on that tree red?" The person replied: "Yes, sir." The other disputant said: "What do you say? It is not red, it is blue." The person again humbly replied: "Yes, sir." The person knew that the chameleon is an animal which constantly changes color; thus it was that he said "yes" to both these conflicting statements. The *Satchitananda* (the Absolute Existence-Intelligence-Bliss) likewise has many forms. The devotee who has seen God in one aspect only, knows Him in that aspect alone. But he who has seen Him in manifold aspects is alone in a position to say with authority: "All these forms are of one God and God is multiform." He is formless and with form, and many are His forms which no one knows. (pp. 28-30)

4.3 — The Guru and the Student

Swami Vivekananda

The Need for a Guru

Every soul is destined to be perfect, and every being, in the end, will attain the state of perfection. Whatever we are now is the result of our acts and thoughts in the past; and whatever we shall be in the future will be the result of what we think and do now. But this, the shaping of our own destinies, does not preclude our receiving help from outside; nay, in the vast majority of cases such help is absolutely necessary. When it comes, the higher powers and possibilities of the soul are quickened, spiritual life is awakened, growth is animated, and man becomes holy and perfect in the end.

This quickening impulse cannot be derived from books. The soul can only receive impulses from another soul, and from nothing else. We may study books all our lives, we may become very intellectual, but in the end we find that we have not developed at all spiritually. It is not true that a high order of intellectual development always goes hand in hand with a proportionate development of the spiritual side in Man. In studying books we are sometimes deluded into thinking that thereby we are being spiritually helped; but if we analyse the effect of the study of books on ourselves, we shall find that at the utmost it is only our intellect that derives profit from such studies, and not our inner spirit. This inadequacy of books to quicken spiritual growth is the reason why, although almost every one of us can *speak* most wonderfully on spiritual matters, when it comes to action and the living of a truly spiritual life, we find ourselves so awfully deficient. To quicken the spirit, the impulse must come from another soul.

The person from whose soul such impulse comes is called the Guru — the teacher; and the person to whose soul the impulse is conveyed is called the Shishya—the student. To convey such an impulse to any soul, in the first place, the soul from which it proceeds must possess the power of transmitting it, as it were, to another; and in the second place, the soul to which it is transmitted must be fit to receive it. The seed must be a living seed, and the field must be ready ploughed; and when both these condi-

Swami Vivekananda. "Bhakti Yoga." *The Four Yogas*. New York: SophiaOmni Press, 2017.

tions are fulfilled, a wonderful growth of genuine religion takes place.

"The true preacher of religion has to be of wonderful capabilities, and clever shall his hearer be"—and when both of these are really wonderful and extraordinary, then will a splendid spiritual awakening result, and not otherwise. Such alone are the real teachers, and such alone are also the real students, the real aspirants. All others are only playing with spirituality. They have just a little curiosity awakened, just a little intellectual aspiration kindled in them, but are merely standing on the outward fringe of the horizon of religion.

There is no doubt some value even in that, as it may in course of time result in the awakening of a real thirst for religion; and it is a mysterious law of nature that as soon as the field is ready, the seed *must* and does come; as soon as the soul earnestly desires to have religion, the transmitter of the religious force *must* and does appear to help that soul. When the power that attracts the light of religion in the receiving soul is full and strong, the power which answers to that attraction and sends in light does come as a matter of course.

Dangers to the Student and the Teacher

There are, however, certain great dangers in the way. There is, for instance, the danger to the receiving soul of its mistaking momentary emotions for real religious yearning. We may study that in ourselves. Many a time in our lives, somebody dies whom we loved; we receive a blow; we feel that the world is slipping between our fingers, that we want something surer and higher, and that we must become religious. In a few days that wave of feeling has passed away, and we are left stranded just where we were before.

We are all of us often mistaking such impulses for real thirst after religion; but as long as these momentary emotions are thus mistaken, that continuous, real craving of the soul for religion will not come, and we shall not find the true transmitter of spirituality into our nature. So whenever we are tempted to complain of our search after the truth that we desire so much, proving vain, instead of so complaining, our first duty ought to be to look into our own souls and find whether the craving in the heart is real. Then in the vast majority of cases it would be discovered that we were not fit for receiving the truth, that there was no real thirst for spirituality.

There are still greater dangers in regard to the *transmitter*, the Guru. There are many who, though immersed in ignorance, yet, in the pride of their hearts, fancy they know everything, and not only do not stop there, but offer to take others on their shoulders; and thus the blind leading the blind, both fall into the ditch. "Fools dwelling in darkness, wise in their own conceit, and puffed up with vain knowledge, go round and round staggering to and fro, like blind men led by the blind." (Katha Up., I. ii. 5).

The world is full of these. Every one wants to be a teacher, every beggar wants to make a gift of a million dollars! Just as these beggars are ridiculous, so are these teachers.

Qualifications of the Student and Teacher

How are we to know a teacher, then? The sun requires no torch to make him visible, we need not light a candle in order to see him. When the sun rises, we instinctively become aware of the fact, and when a teacher of men comes to help us, the soul will instinctively know that truth has already begun to shine upon it. Truth stands on its own evidence, it does not require any other testimony to prove it true, it is self-effulgent. It penetrates into the innermost corners of our nature, and in its presence the whole universe stands up and says, "This is truth."

The teachers whose wisdom and truth shine like the light of the sun are the very greatest the world has known, and they are worshipped as God by the major portion of mankind. But we may get help from comparatively lesser ones also; only we ourselves do not possess intuition enough to judge properly of the man from whom we receive teaching and guidance; so there ought to be certain tests, certain conditions, for the teacher to satisfy, as there are also for the taught.

Qualifications for the Student

The conditions necessary for the taught are purity, a real thirst after knowledge, and perseverance. No impure soul can be really religious. Purity in thought, speech, and act is absolutely necessary for anyone to be religious. As to the thirst after knowledge, it is an old law that we all get whatever we want. None of us can get anything other than what we fix our hearts upon. To pant for religion truly is a very difficult thing, not at all so easy as we generally imagine. Hearing religious talks or reading religious books is no proof yet of a real want felt in the heart; there must be a continuous struggle, a constant fight, an unremitting grappling with our lower nature, till the higher want is actually felt and the victory is achieved. It is not a question of one or two days, of years, or of lives; the struggle may have to go on for hundreds of lifetimes. The success sometimes may come immediately, but we must be ready to wait patiently even for what may look like an infinite length of time. The student who sets out with such a spirit of perseverance will surely find success and realisation at last.

Qualifications for the Teacher

In regard to the teacher, we must see that he knows the spirit of the scriptures. The whole world reads Bibles, Vedas, and Korans; but they are all only words, syntax, etymology, philology, the dry bones of religion. The teacher who deals too much in words and allows the mind to be carried away by the force of words loses the spirit. It is the knowledge of the spirit of the scriptures alone that constitutes the true religious teacher. The network of the words of the scriptures is like a huge forest in which the human mind often loses itself and finds no way out.

"The network of words is a big forest; it is the cause of a curious wandering of the mind."

"The various methods of joining words, the various methods of speaking in beautiful language, the various methods of explaining the diction of the scriptures are only for the disputations and enjoyment of the learned, they do not conduce to the development of spiritual perception."

Those who employ such methods to impart religion to others are only desirous to show off their learning, so that the world may praise them as great scholars. You will find that no one of the great teachers of the world ever went into these various explanations of the text; there is with them no attempt at 'text-torturing', no eternal playing upon the meaning of words and their roots. Yet they nobly taught, while others who have nothing to teach have taken up a word sometimes and written a three-volume book on its origin, on the man who used it first, and on what that man was accustomed to eat, and how long he slept, and so on.....

The second condition necessary in the teacher is — sinlessness. The question is often asked, "Why should we look into the character and personality of a teacher? We have only to judge of what he says, and take that up." This is not right. If a man wants to teach me something of dynamics, or chemistry, or any other physical science, he may be anything he likes, because what the physical sciences require is merely an intellectual equipment; but in the spiritual sciences it is impossible from first to last that there can be any spiritual light in the soul that is impure. What religion can an impure man teach? The sine qua non of acquiring spiritual truth for one's self or for imparting it to others is the purity of heart and soul. A vision of God or a glimpse of the beyond never comes until the soul is pure.

Hence with the teacher of religion we must see first what he is, and then what he says. He must be perfectly pure, and then alone comes the value of his words, because he is only then the true "transmitter." What can he transmit if he has not spiritual power in himself? There must be the worthy vibration of spirituality in the mind of the teacher, so that it may be sympathetically conveyed to the mind of the taught. The function of the teacher is indeed an affair of the transference of something, and not one of mere stimulation of the existing intellectual or other faculties in the taught. Something real and appreciable as an influence comes from the teacher and goes to the taught. Therefore the teacher must be pure.

The third condition is in regard to the motive. The teacher must not teach with any ulterior selfish motive — for money, name, or fame; his work must be simply out of love, out of pure love for mankind at large. The only medium through which spiritual force can be transmitted is love. Any selfish motive, such as the desire for gain or for name, will immediately destroy this conveying median. God is love, and only he who has known God as love can be a teacher of godliness and God to man.

When you see that in your teacher these conditions are all fulfilled, you are safe; if they are not, it is unsafe to allow yourself to be taught by him, for there is the great danger that, if he cannot convey goodness to your heart, he may convey wickedness. This danger must by all means be guarded against. "He who is learned in the scriptures, sinless, unpolluted by lust, and is the greatest knower of the Brahman" is the real teacher.

4.4 — Worshipping the Lord

Bhagavata Purana 11.27

[1] Uddhava said, "My Lord, please explain to me the proper method for worshipping you as a divine being?"...

[7] The Supreme Lord said, "One should worship me by one of three methods: Vedic, Tantric, and mixed. [8] Now listen carefully as I explain exactly how a man who has attained twice-born status according to Vedic precepts should worship me with devotion. [9] One with a pure heart should worship me, his Lord, with the appropriate materials, as an image—that is, as symbol drawn on the ground, in fire, in the sun, in water, or in his own heart.

[10] At sunrise, one should purify his body by bathing and brushing his teeth. While uttering Vedic and Trantric mantras, he should then rub his body with earth to cleanse it. [11] To free himself from the bondage of karma, he should then perform the morning ritual and other rites specified in the Vedas.

[12] My images are of eight types: in stone, wood, metal, clay, painting, sand, precious gems, and images kept in the mind.

[13] My spirit dwells in images of two kinds—the permanent and the temporary. But a permanent deity, having been brought forth, Oh Uddhava, can never be sent away. [14] A deity that is temporarily established—as with an image traced upon the ground—can be called forth and sent away. Cleansing of an image can be done with water, unless the image is made of (smearable substances like) clay, paint or wood, in which case, cleansing should be done without water. [15] Worship me in the form of images using the most excellent materials available, but a devotee with a pure heart may worship me with whatever materials are available and may even worship me mentally in his heart.

[16] When I am worshipped as an image in a temple, bathing and decorating me are most pleasing to me; for a deity traced on the ground, these deities should be positioned in proper places with the appropriate mantras; when I am worshipped in the sacrificial fire, offerings soaked in ghee (clarified butter) are preferred; when worshipped in the sun, prostrations and hymns are best; when worship is offered in water, the offering of water itself I liked by me. [17] For even water, offered with love by a devotee, pleases me.

The Bhagavata Purana 11.27. Trans. A.J. Grunthaler.

[18] But even the most elaborate offerings of flowers, incense perfume, and food, offered without proper devotion, do not please me....

[19] After having cleansed himself and having gathered the appropriate materials for worship, the devotee should arrange to sit on some darbha grass, whose tips point eastward. He should sit facing east or north, or, in the case of a fixed deity image, he should sit directly facing the deity. [20] He should then utter the sacred mantras while sanctifying various parts of his body. Doing the same for my deity image, he should cleanse my image of previously offered materials such as old flowers, and prepare the sacred pot and water vessels for the sprinkling. [21] Then, with the water from that pot, he should sprinkle the area where the deity is bring worshipped, the offerings presented, and his own body. Next, he should decorate the three vessels filled with water with auspicious items available.

[22] Then the devotee should purify those three vessels. He chants the three [appropriate] mantras [for each vessel] and sanctifies them all by chanting the Gayatri mantra. [23] He should then meditate on my subtle form in his own body now purified by air and fire. This is the form of Lord of all beings, who is experienced by sages as they meditate upon the last vibration of the sacred syllable OM. [24] When the devotee's entire being has been pervaded by my form, recognized as being identical to his own Self, then the devotee becomes completely absorbed in Me. Making my presence overflow into the image in front of him, the devotee may now offer me worship.

[25] The devotee first imagines my seat as comprised of nine elements....[26] Then, using Vedic and Tantric mantras, he should make offerings unto me with water for washing the feet, water for washing the mouth..., and other items for worship. By doing so, he attains benefits now and in the hereafter....

[30] The devotee should bathe my image every day using [scented] water... while chanting [the appropriate] mantras..... [32] He should then decorate this image with clothing, sacred threads, ornaments...and garlands. [33] In a spirit of faith, my devotee should offer me water for washing, fragrant oil, flowers, and unbroken rice, incense, lamps, and other items. [34] If it possible according to his means, he should make offerings of food like candy, sweet rice, ghee, rice cakes, etc., On festival days, he should offer annointings, oil massage..., and entertainments involving song and dance....

[48] One should most certainly worship me in my sacred image—or anywhere, for I abide in all things.... [49] By adoring me according to Vedic and Tantric rites, one obtains blessings in this life as well as in the next.

[50] In order to properly establish my deity, one should build a temple for me with fragrant flower gardens to provide flowers for regular worship and festivals.... [52] By making images, one gains the earth; by building a

temple, one gains the three worlds; by performing rituals and services unto me, he gains the world of Brahma. But when he does all three, he gains equality with me. [53] For I am attained through the practice of devotion (Bhakti Yoga)…"

 **4.5 — Mystical Ecstasy**

The Songs of Kabir

Kabir was a 15th century Indian mystic and poet. Although born into a Muslim household, he became influenced by the Hindu bhakti teacher Ramananda. He wrote numerous poems in Hindi, which were originally transmitted orally and only written down in the 17th century. Although he was influenced by both Hinduism and Islam, Kabir was critical of both religions, rejecting their over-emphasis on ritual.

O servant, where do you seek Me?
  Look! I am beside you.
I am neither in temple nor in mosque: I am neither in Kaaba nor in
  Kailash:
Neither am I in rites and ceremonies, nor in Yoga and renunciation.
If you are a true seeker, you shall at once see Me: you shall meet Me in a
  moment of time.
Kabir says, "O Sadhu! God is the breath of all breath."

So long as man clamours for the *I* and the *Mine*, his works are nothing:
When all love of the *I* and the *Mine* is dead, then the work of the Lord is
  done.
For work has no other aim than the getting of knowledge:
When that comes, then work is put away.

When He Himself reveals Himself, Brahma brings into manifestation
That which can never be seen.
As the seed is in the plant, as the shade is in the tree, as the void is in the
  sky, as infinite forms are in the void—
So from beyond the Infinite, the Infinite comes; and from the Infinite the
  finite extends.

The creature is in Brahma, and Brahma is in the creature: they are ever
  distinct, yet ever united.
He Himself is the tree, the seed, and the germ.

———

Songs of Kabir. Trans. Rabindranath Tagore. New York: Macmillan, 1915. Translation updated.

He Himself is the flower, the fruit, and the shade.
He Himself is the sun, the light, and the lighted.
He Himself is Brahma, creature, and Maya.
He Himself is the manifold form, the infinite space;
He is the breath, the word, and the meaning.
He Himself is the limit and the limitless: and beyond both the limited and
    the limitless is He, the Pure Being.
He is the Immanent Mind in Brahma and in the creature.

The Supreme Soul is seen within the soul,
The Point is seen within the Supreme Soul,
And within the Point, the reflection is seen again.
Kabir is blest because he has this supreme vision!

O My heart! the Supreme Spirit, the great Master, is near you: wake, oh
    wake!
Run to the feet of your Beloved: for
    your Lord stands near to your head.
You have slept for unnumbered ages; this morning will you not wake?

Lamps burn in every house, O blind one! and you cannot see them.
One day your eyes shall suddenly be opened, and you shall see: and the
    fetters of death will fall from you.
There is nothing to say or to hear, there is nothing to do: it is he who is
    living, yet dead, who shall never die again.

More than all else do I cherish at heart that love which makes me to live
    a limitless life in this world.
It is like the lotus, which lives in the water and blooms in the water: yet
    the water cannot touch its petals, they open beyond its reach.
It is like a wife, who enters the fire at the bidding of love. She burns and
    lets others grieve, yet never dishonours love.
This ocean of the world is hard to cross: its waters are very deep. Kabir
    says: "Listen to me, O Sadhu! few there are who have reached its end."

My Lord hides Himself, and my Lord wonderfully reveals Himself:
My Lord has encompassed me with hardness, and my Lord has cast
    down my limitations.
My Lord brings to me words of sorrow and words of joy, and He Himself
    heals their strife.
I will offer my body and mind to my Lord: I will give up my life, but
    never can I forget my Lord!

All things are created by the Om;
The love-form is His body.
He is without form, without quality, without decay:
Seek union with Him!
But that formless God takes a thousand forms in the eyes of His
    creatures:
He is pure and indestructible,
His form is infinite and fathomless,
He dances in rapture, and waves of form arise from His dance.
The body and the mind cannot contain themselves, when they are
    touched by His great joy.
He is immersed in all consciousness, all joys, and all sorrows;
He has no beginning and no end;
He holds all within His bliss.

Dance, my heart! Dance today with joy.
The strains of love fill the days and the nights with music, and the world
    is listening to its melodies:
Mad with joy, life and death dance to the rhythm of this music. The hills
    and the sea and the earth dance. The world of man dances in laughter
    and tears.
Why put on the robe of the monk, and live aloof from the world in lonely
    pride?
Behold! my heart dances in the delight of a hundred arts; and the Creator
    is well pleased.

Where is the need of words, when love has made drunken the heart?
I have wrapped the diamond in my cloak; why open it again and again?
When its load was light, the pan of the balance went up: now it is full,
    where is the need for weighing?
The swan has taken its flight to the lake beyond the mountains; why
    should it search for the pools and ditches any more?
Your Lord dwells within you: why need your outward eyes be opened?
Kabir says: "Listen, my brother! my Lord, who ravishes my eyes, has
    united Himself with me."

O Sadhu! the simple union is the best. Since the day when I met with my
Lord, there has been no end to the sport of our love.
I shut not my eyes, I close not my ears, I do not mortify my body;
I see with eyes open and smile, and behold His beauty everywhere:
I utter His Name, and whatever I see, it reminds me of Him; whatever I
    do, it becomes His worship.

The rising and the setting are one to me; all contradictions are solved.
Wherever I go, I move round Him,
All I achieve is His service:
When I lie down, I lie prostrate at His feet.

He is the only adorable one to me: I have none other.
My tongue has left off impure words, it sings His glory day and night:
Whether I rise or sit down, I can never forget Him; for the rhythm of His
   music beats in my ears.
Kabir says: "My heart is frenzied, and I disclose in my soul what is
   hidden. I am immersed in that one great bliss which transcends all
   pleasure and pain."

There is a strange tree, which stands without roots and bears fruits
   without blossoming;
It has no branches and no leaves, it is lotus all over.
Two birds sing there; one is the Guru, and the other the disciple:
The disciple chooses the manifold fruits of life and tastes them, and the
Guru beholds him in joy.
What Kabir says is hard to understand: "The bird is beyond seeking, yet
   it is most clearly visible. The Formless is in the midst of all forms. I
   sing the glory of forms."

Subtle is the path of love!
Therein there is no asking and no not-asking,
There one loses one's self at His feet,
There one is immersed in the joy of the seeking: plunged in the deeps of
   love as the fish in the water.
The lover is never slow in offering his head for his Lord's service.
Kabir declares the secret of this love.

He is the real Sadhu, who can reveal the form of the Formless to the
   vision of these eyes:
Who teaches the simple way of attaining Him, that is other than rites or
   ceremonies:
Who does not make you close the doors, and hold the breath, and
   renounce the world:
Who makes you perceive the Supreme Spirit wherever the mind attaches
   itself:
Who teaches you to be still in the midst of all your activities.
Ever immersed in bliss, having no fear in his mind, he keeps the spirit of
   union in the midst of all enjoyments.

The infinite dwelling of the Infinite Being is everywhere: in earth, water,
   sky, and air:
Firm as the thunderbolt, the seat of the seeker is established above the
   void.
He who is within is without: I see Him and none else.

The Yogi dyes his garments, instead of dyeing his mind in the colors of
   love:
He sits within the temple of the Lord, leaving Brahma to worship a stone.
He pierces holes in his ears, he has a great beard and matted locks, he
   looks like a goat:
He goes forth into the wilderness, killing all his desires, and turns himself
   into an eunuch:
He shaves his head and dyes his garments; he reads the Gita and becomes
   a mighty talker.
   Kabir says: "You are going to the doors of death, bound hand and
   foot!"

Serve your God, who has come into this temple of life!
Do not act the part of a madman, for the night is thickening fast.
He has awaited me for countless ages, for love of me He has lost His
   heart:
Yet I did not know the bliss that was so near to me, for my love was not
   yet awake.
But now, my Lover has made known to me the meaning of the note that
   struck my ear:
Now, my good fortune is come.
Kabir says: "Behold! how great is my good fortune! I have received the
   unending caress of my Beloved!"

PRACTICES

Devotional Mantras

A mantra or mantram, as we've seen, is a sacred word that is repeated silently over and over. In Bhakti Yoga, the mantras that are typically used symbolize the presence of the divinity within ourselves. The repetition of the mantra focuses the mind, calms it down, and allows the presence of the divinity within ourselves to become manifested.

In his *Mantram Handbook* (Nilgiri Press, 2008) Eknath Easwaran provides two pieces of advice for choosing an appropriate mantra (assuming that you don't a guru or teacher to give you one): First, choose a mantra that doesn't have negative baggage for you. For example, it probably wouldn't be a good idea for a lapsed Christian to choose "Lord have mercy." But a less theistically-loaded mantra like, "Om mani padme hum" (a common Buddhist mantra) or "Om, Shanti, Shanti, Shanti" (The Peace Mantra) would probably be fine. Second, rather than making up your own mantra, Easwaran says that it's better to choose a traditional one that has proven power.

Repetition is key when using a mantra, so you should turn to it often during the course of your day: when you're waiting on line at the Post Office, when you're stressed out before an exam, when you're taking a shower. The mantra should be repeated as often as possible in order to sink fully into your consciousness. And once you have chosen your mantra, it's important to stick with it. Ideally, the same mantra should be used throughout the course of a person's life. As Mahatma Gandhi once said, *"The mantra becomes one's staff of life, and carries one through every ordeal. It is no empty repetition. For each repetition has a new meaning, carrying you nearer and nearer to God."*

There are those who say that a mantra should only be given to you by a guru who is him- or herself fairly self-realized and that your mantra should always be kept secret from others. These sorts of requirements may be ideal, but they're hardly necessary. Apart from any spiritual effects, the repetition of any mantra has been shown to have enormous psychological benefits (calming of the mind, improved concentration, reduction of stress). And you don't necessarily have to be a very religious person to reap these benefits.

Finally, any mantra that you choose can also be practiced as a chant before, after, or in place of your daily meditative practice. Instead of repeating the words in your mind, you say them out loud for a set period of time. The key in chanting is to invest yourself fully in the spirit of the chant and not to allow the rational mind to interfere too much in what you are doing.

COMMON MANTRAS

Hindu

Rama [Rah-mah]
("God." Gandhi's mantra)

Haré Rama, Haré Rama [Ha-re Ra-ma, Ha-re Ra-ma]
Rama Rama, Haré Haré [Ra-ma Ra-ma, Ha-re Ha-re]
Haré Krishna, Haré Krishna [Ha-re Krish-na, Ha-re Krish-na]
Krishna Krishna, Haré Haré [Krish-na Krish-na, Ha-re Har-re]

Om Sri Ram, jai Ram, jai jai Ram Om [Om Shree Ram, Jay Ram, Jay, Jay Ram Om]
("Beloved Ram, I honor You;" "May the Lord that dwells in my heart be triumphant over all obstacles.")

Om Namah Shivaya [Ohm Nah-mah Shee-vah-yah]
("I bow to Shiva;" "I honor the Divinity within myself").

Om, Shanti, Shanti, Shanti [Ohm Shawn-tee, Shawn-tee, Shawn-tee]
(The Peace Mantra; An invocation to eternal peace)

Buddhist

Om mani padme hum [Ohm Mah-nee Pahd-may Hume]
("The jewel in the lotus of the heart")

Namo Butsaya [Nah-mo Boot-sie-yah]
("I bow to the Buddha')

Atta Dipa Viharatha (or just Atta Dipa) [at-ta di-pa vi-ha-ra-tha]
("Be a light unto yourself")

Christian

Lord Jesus Christ have mercy on me
(Known as the Jesus Prayer from *The Way of the Pilgrim*)

Kyrie eleison [Kir-ee-ay Ee-lay-ee-sone]
("Lord have mercy." Short form of the Jesus Prayer in Greek)

Deus meus et omnia [de-yus me-yus et om-ni-uh]
("My God and my all." Used by Saint Francis of Assisi)

Maranatha (Mar-ah-nah-tha)
("Come O Lord")

Hail Mary, full of grace.

Jewish

Barukh attah Adonai [Bah-rookh At-tah Ah-doh-nigh]
("Blessed art thou, O Lord")

Muslim

Allahu akbar [Ah-lah-oo Ah-bahr]
("God is great")

5
KARMA YOGA

We've seen that liberation can be attained through the paths of Self-knowledge and devotion. But in Hinduism it can also be attained through selfless action in the world—through the practice of Karma Yoga. In the *Bhagavad Gita* Karma Yoga is called the optimal path for those who are not temperamentally inclined to philosophical reflection or meditation:

> Still your mind in me, still your intellect in me, and without doubt you will be united with me forever. If you cannot still your mind in me, learn to do so through the regular practice of meditation. If you lack the will for such self-discipline, engage yourself in my work, for selfless service can lead you to complete fulfillment. If you are unable to do even this, surrender yourself to me, disciplining yourself and renouncing the results of all your actions.[1]

The practice of Karma Yoga specifically involves performing one's actions selflessly—or to put this in more traditional language, without any thought to the "fruits of action." These fruits, or results of action, can be positive or negative. According to the teachings of Karma Yoga, by focusing on results, all we do is satisfy the ego, which creates attachment and suffering. But, by acting without concern for the results of our actions we begin to transcend ego, which moves us along the path to liberation.

We've seen that Jnana Yoga is mainly monistic in its approach to reality and that Bhakti Yoga is totally dualistic. So what about Karma Yoga? The answer is that the metaphysics underlying Karma Yoga can take many different forms: It can be dualistic when the aim is devotion to a particular deity; it can be monistic when the aim is self-realization; it can even be agnostic or atheistic if the aim is to do good for its own sake.[2]

Swami Sivananda, founder of the Divine Life Society, maintains that

Karma Yoga is totally compatible with the three other forms of yoga. Furthermore, he says, it actually lays the foundation for the practice of each of the other yogas:

> It must be remembered that Karma, Bhakti, and Jnana do not mutually exclude each other. Karma Yoga leads to Bhaki Yoga which in turn leads to Raja Yoga. Raja Yoga beings Jnana… Every Yoga is a fulfillment of the preceeding one. Bhakti is the fulfillment of Karma, [Raja] of Bhakti and Karma, and Jnana of all the preceeding three.[3]

Although one might quibble with Swami Sivananda's hierarchical understanding of the four yogas, his observation that Karma Yoga can be seen as a foundational practice within the other yogic systems is totally valid. There is nothing contradictory—and indeed nothing harmful at all—with practicing Karma Yoga at the same time as Bhakti, Raja, or Jnana Yoga. In fact, the addition of this practice would undoubtedly strengthen the other practices. As Sivanada observes, the *jnani* who focuses exclusively on the attainment of Self-knowledge and who doesn't engage in any kind of selfless service to his fellow man may actually undermine his entire practice by practicing what is essentially a merely conceptual form of religion.[4]

The Cause of Bondage

Our basic problem as human beings is that we continually engage in selfish actions—what Swami Vivekananda calls the "feeling of 'I and Mine.'"[5] Unfortunately, our selfish actions produce negative karmic effects and lead ultimately to bondage. The cause of our bondage is attachment to the results of our actions: that which is perceived as pleasurable or pleasant to us is regarded as good and that which is perceived as painful or unpleasant is regarded as bad. This leads to craving and eventually our craving becomes habitual.

As we've seen, the word "*karma*" in Sanskrit simply means "action." In Hindu thought our actions shape who we are and what we are to become. Our actions affect us, in other words, in this life and in future lives as well. But action itself is always a result of intention. Good actions are the result of good intentions and bad actions are the result of bad intentions. So we ultimately become what our intentions are. If out intentions are motivated by egoism or selfishness, this generates negative karmic effects that impact us in this life as well as in any future lives.

Selection 5.1 — Selfishness and Human Suffering

The Solution: The Practice of Karma Yoga

Thus, the problem that we encounter as human beings is that every action produces a result and creates a chain of bondage for the one performing it. One might think, then, that the solution to this problem is not to act at all—to try to renounce activity itself. But this is not feasible. In the *Bhagavad Gita* 3.5, for example, Krishna tells Arjuna that the renunciation of activity is impossible, since life itself is activity. We can't just not act. Even the renunciate who abandons the world completely is still acting and is still bound by the karmic effects of their actions. As Georg Feuerstein observes, "So long as the ego…presumes itself to be the author behind actions or inactions, these actions or inactions have a binding power. This reinforces the ego and thereby obstructs the event of enlightenment. Egoic action or inaction generates karma."[6]

If the cause of bondage lies in actions, then Karma Yoga posits that the cure for this bondage must lie in action as well—in selfless action. We are called literally to self-surrender or to transcend the egoistic motivations that typically underlie our actions.

But what makes an act selfless? The simple answer is that a selfless act is one that is performed with complete detachment and equanimity. We act completely for the sake of duty with no regards to the "fruits" of our actions. These fruits or consequences can be positive—involving praise, reward, success, etc.—or they can be negative—involving censure, punishment, or seeming failure—but our attitude in either case remains the same: we remain unmoved and uninfluenced by the potential consequences of performing our various duties in life.

But how does one know where his or her duty lies?

The traditional answer in Hinduism, as we've seen, is that one's duties are directly related to the specific caste (*varna*) to which one belongs and one's particular stage of life (*ashrama*). A text like the *Manusmriti* (*Laws of Manu*), for example, gives fairly explicit instructions for members of each of the four castes on how to fulfill their various duties at various stages in their lives. Similarly, in the *Bhagavad Gita*, Arjuna is admonished to follow his *dharma* as a warrior and wage battle against his enemies. Thus, one fulfills one's duty by acting in accordance with one's *sva-dharma*— one's own particular *dharma* in life. And this will vary somewhat from person to person depending upon one's caste and stage of life.

A broader understanding of where one's duty lies is found in the idea of *"sadharana dharmas"* (universal or common duties). In the *Mahabharata*, for example, the sage Bhishma is asked to define the duties that apply to all human beings regardless of their caste. He replies with nine universal duties: (1) the suppression of anger, (2) truthfulness of speech, (3) justice, (4) forgiveness, (5) begetting children in marriage, (6) purity of conduct, (7) avoidance of quarrel, (8) simplicity, (9) and maintenance of dependents.[7] Thus, we see that there are certain universal codes of behavior that apply in Hinduism regardless of one's station in life.

In a still broader sense, an act can be considered selfless if we focus on the welfare of *all* other human beings—and possibly even *all* sentient beings—when acting and not think about our own self-interest or benefit. As a general practice, Karma yoga in practice could involve shoveling a neighbor's sidewalk after a particularly heavy snowfall or serving others during holidays without expecting a thank you. Or it might involve the far more momentous decision to work to alleviate poverty in one's society or even the world. Or, in the case of a truly self-realized individual, it might even involve the decision to sacrifice your very life for the welfare of another.

Whether one actually accomplishes such noble goals or is recognized at all for his efforts is of no significance to the dedicated *karma yogi*. Remember, the *karma yogi* is called to renounce all possible fruits of his actions. The success or failure of his efforts is completely irrelevant.

The Benefits of Karma Yoga

Actions preformed selflessly—with no desire for reward or even acknowledgement—have a twofold transformative impact: they benefit the world and they benefit the one performing these acts.

It seems evident that acts performed selflessly create a more just and humane social order. If we look at those men and women throughout our human history who have left a truly positive mark on the world—individuals like the Buddha, Jesus, Gandhi, Martin Luther King, Jr., and Mother Teresa—one thing that they all seem to have in common is their willingness to serve others selflessly. On the other hand, individuals like Caesar, Napoleon, or Joseph Stalin, who are driven by more egotistical motivations, certainly leave their mark on history, but the "benefits" of their deeds tend to be ephemeral at best. Selfless individuals also provide an example of enlightened living for others.

Selfless acts also produce important benefits for the one performing them. On a very basic level, the performance of selfless actions serves to morally and spiritually improve one's character. Concerning the transformative benefits of selfless action, Swami Sivananda writes:

[B]y doing service you purify your heart. Egotism, hatred, jealousy, the idea of superiority and all the kindred negative qualities will vanish. Humility, pure love, sympathy, tolerance and mercy will be developed. The sense of separateness will be annihilated. Selfishness will be eradicated. You will get a broad and liberal outlook on life. You will begin to feel oneness and unity.[8]

But selfless actions also serve an even higher spiritual end: In Karma Yoga, it is believed that the performance of such actions exhaust the effects of past karma on the mind and prevent the accumulation of new karmic effects. We no longer build up bad karma, because we are no longer acting out of selfish motives. And this leads as effectively to liberation as devotion, Self-knowledge, or meditation.

 Selection 5.2 — The Benefits of Karma Yoga

NOTES

1. *Bhagavad Gita* 12.8-11. Trans. Eknath Easwaran. Tomales CA: Nilgiri Press, 1985.
2. Swami Adiswarananda. *The Four Yogas* (Woodstock, VT: Skylight Paths Publishing, 2006): 63.
3. Swami Sivananda. *Practice of Karma Yoga.* 10th ed. (Tehri-Garhewal, Uttaranchal, IN: Divine Life Society, 2013): 16.
4. Sivnanda, 16.
5. Swami Vivekananda. *The Four Yogas* (New York: SophiaOmni, 2017): 60.
6. George Feuerstein. *The Yoga Tradition* (Prescott, AZ: Hohm Press, 2001): 48.
7. *The Mahabharata* 12.60. Trans. Kisari Mohan Ganguli (1896). See also Troy Wilson Orgon. *The Hindu Quest for the Perfection of Man* (New Delhi: Munshiram Manoharlal Publishers, 1994): 217.
8. Sivananada, 32.

SOURCES

 ## 5.1 — Selfishness and Human Suffering

Swami Vivekananda

A current of water, rushing down of its own nature, falls into a hollow and makes a whirlpool, and after turning around a little there, it emerges again in the form of a free current. Each human life is like that current. It becomes involved in this world of space, time, and causation, whirls around a little, crying out, "My father, my mother, my name, my fame," and so on, and at last emerges out of it and regains its original freedom. The whole universe is doing that. Whether we know it or not, whether we are conscious or unconscious of it, we are all working to get out of the dream of the world. The aim of our experience in the world is to enable us to get out of the whirlpool, and Karma Yoga is the knowledge of the secret of this work.

The whole universe is working for salvation, for liberty. From the atom to the highest being, all are working for one end: liberty of the mind, of the body, of the Spirit. All things are always trying to get freedom, to fly away from bondage. Instead of being knocked about in this universe, we learn from Karma Yoga the secret of work, the method of work, the organizing power of work. A vast mass of energy may be spent in vain if we do not know how to utilize it....

All that you see, the pains and pleasures and miseries of life are but the temporary conditions of this world. Poverty and wealth and happiness are but momentary; they do not belong to our real nature at all. Our nature is far beyond misery and happiness, far beyond every object of the senses. And yet we still must work. Misery comes through attachment to the things of the world, not through work....

The feeling of "I and mine" causes the whole of our misery. With a sense of possession comes selfishness, and selfishness brings on misery. Every act of selfishness or thought of selfishness makes us attached to something, and immediately we are made slaves. Each wave in the mind that says "I and mine" immediately puts a chain around us and makes us

Swami Vivekananda. "Karma Yoga," *The Four Yogas*. New York: SophiaOmni, 2017.

slaves; and the more we say "I and mine," the more slavery grows, and the more misery increases. Therefore, Karma Yoga tells us to enjoy all the beauty of the world, but not to identify ourselves with any of it. Don't say "mine." Don't say "my house," even in your mind, because when you do, you will forget that all belongs to the Lord, that all *is* the Lord. The whole difficulty is there. Do not project that tentacle of selfishness, "I must possess it." As soon as you do, misery will begin.

So Karma Yoga says, first destroy the tendency to project this tentacle of selfishness, and when you have the power of checking it, hold it in and do not allow the mind to get into the ways of selfishness. Then you may go out into the world and work as much as you like. Mix everywhere; go where you please; you will never be contaminated by evil. There is the lotus leaf in the water; the water cannot moisten or stick to it; so will you live in the world. This is called *vairagya*, "non-attachment." Non-attachment is the basis of all the yogas. Non-attachment does not mean anything that we may do in relations to our external body; it is all in the mind. The binding link of "me and mine" is in the mind. If we do not have a link with the body or with the things of the senses, we remain non-attached, wherever and whatever we may be. We must all work diligently in order to attain this blissful state of non-attachment. Karma Yoga teaches us the method that will help us in giving up attachment, though it is indeed very hard.

Here are the two ways of giving up all attachment. One is for those who do not believe in God or in any outside help. They are simply left to work with their own will, with the powers of their mind and discrimination, thinking, "I must be non-attached." However, for those who believe in God, there is another way, which is much less difficult. They offer and dedicate all the fruits of their work to God; they work as worship, and in doing so, they never feel attached to the results. Whatever they see, feel, hear, or do is for God….

Day and night, let us renounce the selfishness of our seeming self until renunciation becomes a habit with us, until it gets into the blood, the nerves, and the brain, until the whole body is every moment obedient to this idea of selflessness. Go then into the world and its battlefields, and amidst the roaring cannon and the din of war you will find yourself free and at peace.

5.1 — The Benefits of Karma Yoga

Swami Vivekananda

Our duty to others means helping others; doing good to the world. Why should we do good to the world? Apparently to help the world, but really to help ourselves. We should always try to help the world, that should be the highest motive in us; but if we consider well, we find that the world does not require our help at all. This world was not made that you or I should come and help it. I once read a sermon in which it was said, "All this beautiful world is very good, because it gives us time and opportunity to help others." Apparently, this is a very beautiful sentiment, but is it not a blasphemy to say that the world needs our help? We cannot deny that there is much misery in it; to go out and help others is, therefore, the best thing we can do, although in the long run, we shall find that helping others is only helping ourselves. As a boy I had some white mice. They were kept in a little box in which there were little wheels, and when the mice tried to cross the wheels, the wheels turned and turned, and the mice never got anywhere. So it is with the world and our helping it. The only help is that we get moral exercise. This world is neither good nor evil; each man manufactures a world for himself. If a blind man begins to think of the world, it is either as soft or hard, or as cold or hot. We are a mass of happiness or misery; we have seen that hundreds of times in our lives. As a rule, the young are optimistic and the old pessimistic. The young have life before them; the old complain their day is gone; hundreds of desires, which they cannot fulfil struggle in their hearts. Both are foolish nevertheless. Life is good or evil according to the state of mind in which we look at it, it is neither by itself. Fire, by itself, is neither good nor evil. When it keeps us warm we say, "How beautiful is fire!" When it burns our fingers, we blame it. Still, in itself it is neither good nor bad. According as we use it, it produces in us the feeling of good or bad; so also is this world. It is perfect. By perfection is meant that it is perfectly fitted to meet its ends. We may all be perfectly sure that it will go on beautifully well without us, and we need not bother our heads wishing to help it.

Yet we must do good; the desire to do good is the highest motive power we have, if we know all the time that it is a privilege to help others. Do not stand on a high pedestal and take five cents in your hand and say,

Swami Vivekananda. "Karma Yoga," *The Four Yogas*. New York: SophiaOmni, 2017.

"Here, my poor man," but be grateful that the poor man is there, so that by making a gift to him you are able to help yourself. It is not the receiver that is blessed, but it is the giver. Be thankful that you are allowed to exercise your power of benevolence and mercy in the world, and thus become pure and perfect. All good acts tend to make us pure and perfect. What can we do at best? Build a hospital, make roads, or erect charity asylums. We may organise a charity and collect two or three millions of dollars, build a hospital with one million, with the second give balls and drink champagne, and of the third let the officers steal half, and leave the rest finally to reach the poor; but what are all these? One mighty wind in five minutes can break all your buildings up. What shall we do then? One volcanic eruption may sweep away all our roads and hospitals and cities and buildings. Let us give up all this foolish talk of doing good to the world. It is not waiting for your or my help; yet we must work and constantly do good, because it is a blessing to ourselves. That is the only way we can become perfect. No beggar whom we have helped has ever owed a single cent to us; we owe everything to him, because he has allowed us to exercise our charity on him. It is entirely wrong to think that we have done, or can do, good to the world, or to think that we have helped such and such people. It is a foolish thought, and all foolish thoughts bring misery. We think that we have helped some man and expect him to thank us, and because he does not, unhappiness comes to us. Why should we expect anything in return for what we do? Be grateful to the man you help, think of him as God. Is it not a great privilege to be allowed to worship God by helping our fellow men? If we were really unattached, we should escape all this pain of vain expectation, and could cheerfully do good work in the world. Never will unhappiness or misery come through work done without attachment. The world will go on with its happiness and misery through eternity....

This world is like a dog's curly tail, and people have been striving to straighten it out for hundreds of years; but when they let it go, it has curled up again. How could it be otherwise? One must first know how to work without attachment, then one will not be a fanatic. When we know that this world is like a dog's curly tail and will never get straightened, we shall not become fanatics. If there were no fanaticism in the world, it would make much more progress than it does now. It is a mistake to think that fanaticism can make for the progress of mankind. On the contrary, it is a retarding element creating hatred and anger, and causing people to fight each other, and making them unsympathetic. We think that whatever we do or possess is the best in the world, and what we do not do or possess is of no value. So, always remember the instance of the curly tail of the dog whenever you have a tendency to become a fanatic. You need not worry or make yourself sleepless about the world; it will go on without you. When you have avoided fanaticism, then alone will you work well. It is the level-headed man, the calm man, of good judgment and cool nerves, of great sympathy and love, who does good work and so does good to himself. The fanatic is foolish and has no sympathy; he can never straighten the world, nor himself become pure and perfect.

To recapitulate the chief points in today's lecture: First, we have to bear in mind that we are all debtors to the world and the world does not owe us anything. It is a great privilege for all of us to be allowed to do anything for the world. In helping the world we really help ourselves. The second point is that there is a God in this universe. It is not true that this universe is drifting and stands in need of help from you and me. God is ever present therein, He is undying and eternally active and infinitely watchful. When the whole universe sleeps, He sleeps not; He is working incessantly; all the changes and manifestations of the world are His. Thirdly, we ought not to hate anyone. This world will always continue to be a mixture of good and evil. Our duty is to sympathise with the weak and to love even the wrongdoer. The world is a grand moral gymnasium wherein we have all to take exercise so as to become stronger and stronger spiritually. Fourthly, we ought not to be fanatics of any kind, because fanaticism is opposed to love. You hear fanatics glibly saying, "I do not hate the sinner. I hate the sin," but I am prepared to go any distance to see the face of that man who can really make a distinction between the sin and the sinner. It is easy to say so. If we can distinguish well between quality and substance, we may become perfect men. It is not easy to do this. And further, the calmer we are and the less disturbed our nerves, the more shall we love and the better will our work be.

PRACTICES

Because *Karma Yoga* is the yoga of action, it is not practiced on a meditation cushion, but in the world. This means you'll have ample opportunities to develop this practice during the course of your day, provided, first, that you make the commitment to try to behave selflessly and, secondly, that you make an effort to find opportunities to practice.

Morning Dedication

A morning dedication or intention is a fine way to ensure that any practices that you are trying to cultivate in life get off to the right start. In this case, the morning dedication is used to make the commitment to behave selflessly. It is used optimally at the beginning of your morning meditation.

Here is just one form the dedication could take:

"Whatever actions I perform today
with my body, speech, or mind,
either intentionally or unintentionally,
I dedicate them completely to the good of others."
(or "I dedicate them completely to God.")

You can also create your own version of this morning dedication:

The Cultivation of Selflessness

For your practice this week, try the following: throughout your day, you'll undoubtedly be presented with numerous opportunities to practice selfless action. Find at least one occasion to do something for someone else with no regard for your own advantage. If possible, try to perform your selfless act without the beneficiary of this act even being aware that you're doing it.

If you're really committed to the path of selfless action, you might also try keeping a log of any selfless acts you perform over a defined period of time—a week or a month perhaps. Afterwards, reflect upon how you feel after performing this act. Does it make you feel happier or more peaceful? Does it help with your relationships with others?

DATE	SELFLESS ACTION

Developing a Compassionate Mind

This is a form of meditative practice that one can do anytime of the day—whether you are at work, school shopping, or doing just about anything.
Here's how it works:

1. Dedicate a period of about 30 minutes out of your day to affirm everyone you encounter, no matter how superficial this encounter may be. (Naturally, this works better if you are out of the house, so if you have no specific plans during this period, you can just take a walk around your neighborhood).
2. Whenever you encounter someone during this period, make the mental intention, "May you be at peace." Or simply say "*shanti*." The key here is to try to make this intention as sincere as possible—to really wish inner peace and happiness for everyone with whom you interact.
3. If you're going for a walk, do the same for people passing by you in cars. (They need peace too.) And don't forget to wish peace to any animals you encounter—birds, squirrels and, yes, even nasty barking dogs.
4. If you encounter a difficult person during the course of your practice—an annoying customer, a petty classmate, your tyrannical boss—you may find it difficult to sincerely wish this person peace, but try to do so anyway. What you'll probably find is that, as a result of this practice, your relationship with difficult people becomes somewhat less onerous over time.

6
RAJA YOGA

The final yogic path that we will explore is Raja Yoga—the yoga of meditation. The term "raja" literally means "king," and therefore Raja Yoga is often referred to in English as "Royal Yoga." This particular yogic path is also sometimes referred to as Ashtanga (eight-limbed) Yoga, because the path to liberation is described in it as having eight distant stages. Since the last three of these stages emphasize the practice of meditation, Raja Yoga is also known as the path of meditation.

For the most part, Raja Yoga has been identified almost exclusively with the *Yoga Sutras* of Patanjali. Unfortunately, we know very little about Patanjali himself. Traditionally, he was identified as the author of the *Mahabhasya*, a text on Sanskrit grammar from the second century BCE, but that idea is largely rejected now. Today, it's more commonly asserted that the *Yoga Sutras* probably come from the second century CE and represent a compilation of fragments from texts from an earlier tradition. As Georg Feuerstein notes, [Patanjali's] own philosophical contribution, as far as can be gauged from the *Yoga-Sutras* itself, was fairly modest. He appears to have been a compiler and systematizer rather than an originator."[1]

Samkhya Philosophy

The philosophical underpinnings of the *Yoga Sutras* are to be found in the ideas of Samkhya philosophy. Samkhya doctrines go back as far as the early *Upanishads*, but were compiled as a philosophical system only later. Samkhya philosophy is actually quite complex, but there are a few key ideas contained within it that are crucial for an understanding of the *Yoga Sutras*.

Samkhya is completely dualistic in nature, recognizing two ultimate—and essentially independent—realities: *purusha* (pure spirit or consciousness) and *prakriti* (matter).

Prakriti or primal matter is the cause of the universe and everything we experience within it—everything that is temporal and impermanent. Essentially, *prakriti* represents anything that can be an object of experience. This includes, of course, all physical objects: stars and planet, rocks, and our own physical bodies. Since the mind and its processes (thoughts, feelings, awareness of sensations, etc.) are understood to be inextricably connected to physical reality, these too are included in the realm of *prakriti*. *Prakriti*, therefore, basically includes everything except for *purusha*.

In order to explain how the multiplicity of things in the universe came from a single source, Samkhya posits three essential qualities—known as *gunas*—that constitute *prakriti*. These *gunas* are *sattva* (illumination, purity, harmony), *rajas* (activity, passion, confusion), and *tamas* (darkness, inertia, sloth). The various combinations of the *gunas* produce different kinds of persons and things.

In the Samykhya system there is an infinite number of *purushas* and these are completely distinct from one another and from *prakriti*. *Purusha* can never be the object of experience: It is the observer (i.e., the witness) and never the observed. As pure consciousness, it is understood to be uncaused, unchanging, unaffected by experience, and unmoved by pleasure or pain.

Although *purusha* is totally independent of *prakriti*, through ignorance (*avidya*), it can come to identify itself mistakenly with objects of *prakriti* such as the intelligence and ego. This leads to the suffering of afflictions and ultimately to rebirth. John M. Koller uses the analogy of a in a room surrounded by audiovisual devices to describe how in Samkhya ignorance inevitably leads to suffering:

> A film projector runs, showing someone picked up out of the sea, wafted to the peak of a jagged cliff high over the water, and plummeted down to be dashed against the rocks below. The viewer who identifies with the victim of this horrible fate suffers. But when the viewer realizes that this suffering self is an illusion created out of mere film and sound, freedom from suffering is achieved.[2]

Liberation in Samkhya, therefore, ultimately comes from the right knowledge (*viveka*) that allows one to perceive the difference between *purusha* and *prakriti*. When this occurs, the Self is no longer bound by *prakriti*, it gains isolation (*kaivalya*), and ultimately achieves liberation (*moksha*).

So much for the basics of Samkhya philosophy. Now we can turn to the ideas in the *Yoga Sutras*.

Structure of the Yoga Sutras

The Sanskrit word "*sutra*" literally means "to thread or weave" and shares a common root with the English word suture, which means "to stitch together." This is probably a good way to understand the *Yoga Sutras*. The work is composed of 196 sutras or aphorisms that are so concise undoubtedly because they served as a mnemonic device for students to help them remember more detailed lecture discussions that were orally transmitted to them by a teacher. S.N. Dasgupta likens these sutras "to lecture hints."[3]

The text itself is divided into four *padas* (literally "foots" or "steps"). In the *Yoga Sutras* this simply refers to the subdivision of the work into four distinct parts or books.

1. Samadhi Pada: The Book on Samadhi
2. Sadhana Pada: The Book on (Yogic) Practice
3. Vibhuti Pada: The Book on (Yogic) Accomplishments
4. Kaivalya Pada: The Book on Liberation

This division of the text, unfortunately, doesn't completely hold up under scrutiny. This is a work that attempts to cobble together ideas possibly developed over centuries and derived from different schools, and consistency of thought, therefore, is occasionally sacrificed.

The Meaning and Aim of Yoga

In the second sutra of the first part of the *Yoga Sutras*, Patanjali defines yoga as "*yogas citta vritti nirodha*." Pages have been written on the meaning and importance of each of these terms, since they encapsulate the entire philosophy of the *Yoga Sutras*. At the very least, therefore, it's important to clarify the meaning of *citta*, *vritti*, and *nirodha* before proceeding any further:

Although many editions of the *Yoga Sutras* translate "*citta*" as mind, this is a bit misleading. There's already a word in Hinduism that corresponds to "mind" and that's "*manas*." The term *citta* is much broader and involves observing, thinking, imagining, reflecting, etc., and is probably best rendered as "consciousness"—or better yet, as embodied consciousness as opposed to pure or Superconsciouness.

The term "*vritti*," which literally means "whirlpool," has been translated as "movements," "fluctuation," "flutterings," or "disturbances." The *vritti* are basically activities of consciousness that are directed towards the realm of *prakriti*. Patanjali identifies five fluctuations of consciousness: true knowledge that is derived from perception, inference or the testimony of authority (*pramana*), error (*viparyaya*), conceptual knowledge or imagination (*vikalpa*), sleep (*nidra*), and memory (*smirti*) (1.5-11). He goes on to observe that these activities of consciousness can either be afflictive (*klista*)—leading to suffering or pain—or non-afflictive (*aklista*)—not leading to suffering or pain.

Nirodha simply means "restraint," or "control."

Putting this all together "*yogas citta vritti nirodha*" can roughly be translated as "Yoga is the stilling of the fluctuations of consciousness." The consciousness of the average person is directed towards an almost limitless number of objects during waking moments—and at times even during sleep. These fluctuations of consciousness that arise as the senses interact with the external world, lead to psychic dispersal, worry, and agitation. What yoga calls for, according to Patanjali, is the stilling of such fluctuations.

The analogy that is commonly used to describe consciousness is that of a pond. When a pond is still, it can be used as a mirror to reflect objects. But when the pond is unsettled by turbulence, the reflected image becomes distorted. The still pond in this analogy represents pure consciousness in which all fluctuations have ceased; the turbulent pond represents the fluctuations of consciousness.

That's all well and good, but what ultimately is the goal of yogic practice? Immediately following his definition of yoga, Patajali says, "When this is accomplished, then the seer abides in his true nature. Otherwise the seer identifies with the fluctuations of consciousness" (1.3-4). Following Samkhya philosophy, Patanjali recognizes the basic problem that human beings have is that they identify their true Selves with the fluctuations of consciousness and this leads to suffering. It therefore follows that, if we can somehow learn to identify with this true Self (aka, Atman, Purusha, Pure Sprit), we can attain liberation.

As Gregor Maehle puts it,

> To abide in one's nature simply means to stop projecting oneself outward. Projecting outward means identifying with the perceived. Giving up this projection is to abide in the core, which implies watching the world and one's body/mind go by. The nature of the seer is awareness. To abide in one's nature as awareness simply means to know that we are awareness and not lose sight of that.[4]

In other words, the aim of yoga, as Patanjali describes it, is to create the conditions whereby we stop identifying ourselves with our mental activities in particular and learn to identify with our true nature, pure awareness or consciousness.

Examining the Causes of Suffering

Let's examine the fluctuations of consciousness a bit further and see how they lead to suffering. The *vritti* are negatively affected by what is known as the five *kleshas*, or afflictions. These five afflictions are ignorance (*avidya*), egotism (*asmita*), attachment (*raga*), aversion (*dvesa*), and the will to live as an embodied being (*abhinivesa*).

The reason that these afflictions are problematic is that they leave a subconscious imprint (*samskara*) behind and they create a habitual chain of action and reaction that determines how we will behave in the future. The attachments that we have towards certain pleasurable things (dessert, sex, money), for example, create a subtle unconscious imprint on our consciousness. This imprint is strengthened and reinforced every time in the future that we give into our desire for the pleasurable thing. In other words, the imprints created by the afflictions are the cause of *karma* and are responsible for our suffering in this life and future lives.

So, if these afflictions are basically the cause of suffering, then they need to be overcome. And the way that they are overcome is through the detachment that comes from practicing the eight limbs of yoga.

The Way Out of Suffering: The Eight Limbs of Yoga

The eight limbs of yoga represent a movement of consciousness from the most external and superficial to the most internal and profound. These limbs are:

1. Moral Restraints (*Yamas*)
2. Personal Observances (*Niyamas*)
3. Posture (*Asana*)
4. Breath Control (*Pranayama*)
5. Withdrawal of the Senses (*Pratyahara*)
6. Concentration (*Dharana*)
7. Contemplation (*Dhyana*)
8. Absorption (*Samadhi*)

Traditionally, these limbs are divided into two categories: the external limbs (moral restraints, personal observances, posture, breath control, and withdrawal of the senses) and the internal limbs (concentration, contemplation, absorption). Michaels, however, divides up these limbs into three subgroupings: (1) Moral Preparation (moral restraints, personal observances), (2) Physical Preparation (posture, breath control, withdrawal of the senses), and (3) Spiritual Preparation (concentration, contemplation, absorption).[5]

1. Moral Restraints (*Yamas*). The *yamas* are ethical rules or moral codes. Moral codes like the one presented by Patanjali are in fact the basis for most forms of spiritual practice. The five *yamas* include:

(1) non-violence or non-harming (*ahimsa*)
(2) non-lying or truthfulness (*satya*)
(3) non-stealing (*asteya*)
(4) sexual restraint (*brahmacarya*)
(5) non-greed (*aparigraha*).

The usual motivations for most of our actions stem from desire and aversion. What the moral restraints try to do is reorient our focus so that now we are taking the well-being of others into consideration before acting. *Ahimsa*, in particular, should guide all of our actions. Taken superficially, *ahimsa* simply means refraining from acts of violence against other human beings, but in practice it means refraining from harming any being in thought, word, or deed.

The goal is to make each of these moral restraints part of one's everyday life. The benefits of observing these moral restrains are that one's own nature becomes purified and interactions with other human beings become more harmonious.

2. Personal Observances (*Niyamas*). If the *yamas* can be described as the "don'ts" of yogic practice, the *niyamas* are the "dos." These include:

(1) purity (of body, mind, and speech) or cleanliness (*saucha*)
(2) contentment (*santosha*)
(3) austerity or discipline (*tapas*)
(4) self-study (*svadhyaya*)
(5) devotion to the Lord (*ishvarapranidhana*)

Both the *yamas* and the *niyamas* are an initial attempt to overcome the conditioning to which we have been subjected to as members of society. From the societal, the technique of yoga then turns to the body in order to overcome its conditioning as well.

3. Posture (*Asana*). Interestingly, when most Westerners think of yoga, the various positions of Hatha Yoga immediately come to mind. When Patanjali talks about posture, however, all he means is a comfortable and steady pose that one can maintain without movement for a period of time. It was only later commentators on Patanjali's text like Vyasa who suggested specific number of postures .[6]

This ability to hold the body still is seen as a prerequisite for doing deep meditation. Yoga presupposes an intimate connection between the body and consciousness. If the body is agitated or restless, it's difficult to achieve the calm necessary to meditate. When the body becomes calm, this facilitates the calming of the mind. The goal, in other words. is to bring the body under the control of consciousness rather than the other way around.

4. Breath Control (*Pranayama*). *Pranayama* is the practice of regulating the flow of breath. Actually, the word *prana* means "life force" or "energy," so what we are really taking about with *pranayama* is actually energy control. As Georg Feuerstein notes, "*Prana*...is not merely the breath. The breath is only an external aspect. Or a form of manifestation, of *prana*, which is the life force that interpenetrates and sustains all life."[7]

Through proper posture, the yogi has begun to reduce the external stimuli that lead to distraction. This in turn enables him to become more in tune with the energy that flows through his body. The regulation of this energy flow through the practice of *pranayama* leads to greater relaxation and the diminishment of the impact of the influence of external stimuli, as well as providing a foundation for concentration.

 Selection 6.1 — Pranayama

5. Withdrawal of the Senses (*Pratyahara*). The turn of consciousness from the external to the internal was begun with posture and breath control. This inward turn culminates with sense-withdrawal. *Pratyahara* is the combination of two Sanskrit words: "*prati*" ("towards") and "*ahara*" ("bring near"). It is the method of withdrawing one's senses from external objects and turning one's attention to the (inner self).   The analogy that is frequently used in yogic literature to describe sense withdrawal is the way a tortoise is able to withdraw its head and limbs into its shell. This technique is described in the *Mahabharata* in the following way:

> Freed from the influence of all pairs of opposites (such as heat and cold, joy and sorrow, etc.), ever existing in their own (original) state, liberated (from attachments), never accepting anything (in gift), [yogis] live in places free from the companionship of wives and children, without others with whom disputes may arise, and favorable to perfect tranquility of heart. There such a person, restraining speech, sits like a piece of wood, crushing all the senses....He has no perception of sound through the ear; no perception of touch through the skin; no perception of form through the eye; no perception of taste through the tongue. He has no perception also of scents

through the organ of smell. Immersed in yoga, he would abandon all things, rapt in meditation. Possessed of great energy of mind, he has no desire for anything that excites the five senses.[8]

Why is the withdrawal of the senses so important in yoga? The answer is that it is impossible to turn inward when one is distracted by the senses—for example, by the cramp in your leg or a car horn honking outside. And so the mediator learns to disengage from sensation, not allowing external objects to distract or enchant him.

Pratyahara marks the transition from the external limbs of yoga to its internal limbs by focusing on the techniques of concentration, contemplation, and absorption. These last three limbs of yoga represent the beginning of meditation and are collectively referred to as "*samyama*"—perfect discipline.

6. Concentration (*Dharana*). The root of the word *dharana* is "dhir," which means to "hold" or "maintain." Concentration involves holding one's mind on a single object. The object being focused on can be an external thing (candle flame), a sound (mantra), the image of a deity, the breath, or a thought in the mind. The meditator then begins to still the agitations of the mind, by giving it something specific to focus upon. The goal is for the mind to become so fixed on the object that it achieves a "one-pointed" (*ekagrata*) state.

The act of concentration is far more difficult than it seems, as anyone who has ever attempted meditation knows full well. One attempts to concentrate on an object, only to find the mind wandering again and again. What is required is the discipline, persistence, and patience to return the mind time and again away from what distracts it and back towards the original object of concentration. Eventually, one becomes able to sustain concentration for longer and longer periods of time and greater levels of calm are experienced.

7. Meditation (*Dhyana*). Whereas with concentration we focus our attention with laser-like precision on a particular object, meditation involves maintaining an uninterrupted or sustained state of concentration on the object:

[D]hyana is the stretching out, or extension of, the *dharana*. *Dharana* is characterized by momentary concentration on an object, and *dhyana* is the extension of that concentration into a flowing process. *Dhyana* is the perfection of the process of habituation in *dharana*—rather than having moments of concentration, now the process becomes continuous and sustained, leading to deeper and more peaceful states of meditation....In *dhyana*, the continuity of fixation on the object is not lost for successively longer periods of time, and so concentration becomes more subtle and engrossing.[9]

It is only when the mind is able to focus without distractions on the object of concentration that true meditation has been achieved. As Edwin Bryan notes, concentration and meditation shouldn't be seen as two separate and distinct practices, but rather as "a continuation and deepening of the same practice" (i.e., concentration).[10]

 Selection 6.2 — Dhyana

8. Absorption (*Samadhi*). Once the agitations of the mind have been supressed, the light of pure or Superconsciouness can shine forth. This is the state of *samadhi*. *Samadhi* literally means "putting together" or "union." It is the state of oneness with the object of meditation.

There are two levels of *samadhi*. In *samadhi* with seed, subject object distinction is eliminated, all fluctuations of the mind have been stilled, and there is consciousness only of the object of meditation. In *samadhi* without seed, the object of consciousness itself is eradicated and there is no longer any influence of *prakriti* on consciousness. This is the state of pure consciousness or Superconsciouness.

What the final three stages of yoga ultimately lead to is "*kaivalya*" or "isolation"—a state that is identical to complete liberation. In this state, the meditator grasps the true nature of the Self (*Purusha*) and the world (*Prakriti*) and discerns the difference between the two.

Reading the Yoga Sutras

All of the above background information has been provided to assist in the reading of Patanjali's *Yoga Sutras*. As we've seen, the 196 aphorisms in the text are extremely concise and, therefore, subject to interpretation. Unfortunately, the commentaries on the text that have been produced over the centuries differ dramatically from one another and usually reflect the particular philosophical or doctrinal bias of the commentator. The problem of correct interpretation is compounded when one encounters the text in languages other than Sanskrit, since there are no exact correlations with English words, for instance.

This makes the *Yoga Sutras* difficult to understand, but also represents a wonderful challenge to the reader. This is most assuredly a text that one can spend a lifetime studying. Those interested in delving further into the ideas contained within *Yoga Sutras* are encouraged to read one or more of the books recommended in the "For Further Reading" section of this work.

Selection 6.3 — The Yoga Sutras

NOTES

1. Georg Feuerstein. *Yoga: The Technology of Ecstasy* (Los Angeles: Jeremy P. Tarcher, 1989): 170.
2. John M. Koller. *Asian Philosophies.* 4th edition (Upper Saddle River, NJ: Prentice Hall, 2002): 60.
3. S.N. Dasgupta. *A History of Indian Philosophy.* Vol. 1 (Delhi: Banarsidass, 1975): 62.
4. Gregor Maehle. *Ashtanga Yoga: Practice and Philosophy* (Novato, CA: New World Library, 2006): 146.
5. Alex Michaels. *Hinduism: Past and Present* (Princeton, NJ: Princeton University Press, 2004): 268.
6. *Yoga-Darsana: The Sutras of Patanjali with the Bhasya of Vyasa.* Trans. Ganganatha Jha (Bombay: Tattva-Vivechaka Press, 1907): 89.
7. Feuerstein, 190.
8. *The Mahabharata* 12.195. Trans. Kisari Mohan Ganguli (Calcutta: Bharata Press, 1896).
9. Stuart Ray Sarbacher and Kevin Kimple. *The Eight Limbs of Yoga: A Handbook for Living Yoga Philosophy* (New York: Northpoint Press, 2015): 60.
10. Edwin F. Bryan. *The Yoga Sutras of Patanjali* (New York: Northpoint Press, 2009): 303.

SOURCES

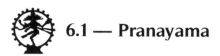 6.1 — Pranayama

Swami Vivekananda

How to control the Prana is the one idea of Pranayama. All the trainings and exercises in this regard are for that one end. Each man must begin where he stands, must learn how to control the things that are nearest to him. This body is very near to us, nearer than anything in the external universe, and this mind is the nearest of all. The Prana which is working this mind and body is the nearest to us of all the Prana in this universe. This little wave of the Prana which represents our own energies, mental and physical, is the nearest to us of all the waves of the infinite ocean of Prana. If we can succeed in controlling that little wave, then alone we can hope to control the whole of Prana. The Yogi who has done this gains perfection; no longer is he under any power....

The Prana is the vital force in every being. Thought is the finest and highest action of Prana. Thought, again, as we see, is not all. There is also what we call instinct or unconscious thought, the lowest plane of action. If a mosquito stings us, our hand will strike it automatically, instinctively. This is one expression of thought. All reflex actions of the body belong to this plane of thought. There is again the other plane of thought, the conscious. I reason, I judge, I think, I see the pros and cons of certain things, yet that is not all. We know that reason is limited. Reason can go only to a certain extent, beyond that it cannot reach. The circle within which it runs is very very limited indeed. Yet at the same time, we find facts rush into this circle. Like the coming of comets certain things come into this circle; it is certain they come from outside the limit, although our reason cannot go beyond. The causes of the phenomena intruding themselves in this small limit are outside of this limit. The mind can exist on a still higher plane, the superconscious. When the mind has attained to that state, which is called Samadhi — perfect concentration, superconsciousness — it goes beyond the limits of reason, and comes face to face with facts which no instinct or reason can ever know. All manipulations of the subtle forces of the body,

Swami Vivekananda. "Raja Yoga." *The Four Yogas*. New York: SophiaOmni, 2017.

the different manifestations of Prana, if trained, give a push to the mind, help it to go up higher, and become superconscious, from where it acts.

In this universe there is one continuous substance on every plane of existence. Physically this universe is one: there is no difference between the sun and you. The scientist will tell you it is only a fiction to say the contrary. There is no real difference between the table and me; the table is one point in the mass of matter, and I another point. Each form represents, as it were, one whirlpool in the infinite ocean of matter, of which not one is constant. Just as in a rushing stream there may be millions of whirlpools, the water in each of which is different every moment, turning round and round for a few seconds, and then passing out, replaced by a fresh quantity, so the whole universe is one constantly changing mass of matter, in which all forms of existence are so many whirlpools. A mass of matter enters into one whirlpool, say a human body, stays there for a period, becomes changed, and goes out into another, say an animal body this time, from which again after a few years, it enters into another whirlpool, called a lump of mineral. It is a constant change. Not one body is constant. There is no such thing as my body, or your body, except in words. Of the one huge mass of matter, one point is called a moon, another a sun, another a man, another the earth, another a plant, another a mineral. Not one is constant, but everything is changing, matter eternally concreting and disintegrating. So it is with the mind. Matter is represented by the ether; when the action of Prana is most subtle, this very ether, in the finer state of vibration, will represent the mind and there it will be still one unbroken mass. If you can simply get to that subtle vibration, you will see and feel that the whole universe is composed of subtle vibrations....

Thus, even in the universe of thought we find unity, and at last, when we get to the Self, we know that that Self can only be One. Beyond the vibrations of matter in its gross and subtle aspects, beyond motion there is but One. Even in manifested motion there is only unity. These facts can no more be denied. Modern physics also has demonstrated that the sum total of the energies in the universe is the same throughout. It has also been proved that this sum total of energy exists in two forms. It becomes potential, toned down, and calmed, and next it comes out manifested as all these various forces; again it goes back to the quiet state, and again it manifests. Thus it goes on evolving and involving through eternity. The control of this Prana, as before stated, is what is called Pranayama.

The most obvious manifestation of this Prana in the human body is the motion of the lungs. If that stops, as a rule all the other manifestations of force in the body will immediately stop. But there are persons who can train themselves in such a manner that the body will live on, even when this motion has stopped. There are some persons who can bury themselves for days, and yet live without breathing. To reach the subtle we must take the help of the grosser, and so, slowly travel towards the most subtle until we gain our point. Pranayama really means controlling this motion of the lungs and this motion is associated with the breath. Not that breath is producing it; on the contrary it is producing breath. This motion draws in the air by pump action. The Prana is moving the lungs, the movement of the lungs draws in the air. So Pranayama is not breathing, but controlling that muscular power which moves the lungs. That muscular power which goes out through the nerves to the muscles and from them to the lungs, making them move in a certain manner, is the Prana, which we have to control in the practice of Pranayama. When the Prana has become controlled, then we shall immediately find that all the other actions of the Prana in the body will slowly come under control. I myself have seen men who have controlled almost every muscle of the body; and why not? If I have control over certain muscles, why not over every muscle and nerve of the body? What impossibility is there? At present the control is lost, and the motion has become automatic. We cannot move our ears at will, but we know that animals can. We have not that power because we do not exercise it. This is what is called atavism.

Again, we know that motion which has become latent can be brought back to manifestation. By hard work and practice certain motions of the body which are most dormant can be brought back under perfect control. Reasoning thus we find there is no impossibility, but, on the other hand. every probability that each part of the body can be brought under perfect control. This the Yogi does through Pranayama. Perhaps some of you have read that in Pranayama, when drawing in the breath, you must fill your whole body with Prana. In the English translations Prana is given as breath, and you are inclined to ask how that is to be done. The fault is with the translator. Every part of the body can be filled with Prana, this vital force, and when you are able to do that, you can control the whole body. All the sickness and misery felt in the body will be perfectly controlled; not only so, you will be able to control another's body. Everything is infectious in this world, good or bad. If your body be in a certain state of tension, it will have a tendency to produce the same tension in others. If you are strong and healthy, those that live near you will also have the tendency to become strong and healthy, but if you are sick and weak, those around you will have the tendency to become the same. In the case of one man trying to heal another, the first idea is simply transferring his own health to the other. This is the primitive sort of healing. Consciously or unconsciously, health can be transmitted. A very strong man, living with a weak man, will make him a little stronger, whether he knows it or not. When consciously done, it becomes quicker and better in its action. Next come those cases in which a man may not be very healthy himself, yet we know that he can bring health to another. The first man, in such a case, has a little more control over the Prana, and can rouse, for the time being, his Prana, as it were, to a certain state of vibration, and transmit it to another person....

The gigantic will-powers of the world, the world-movers, can bring their Prana into a high state of vibration, and it is so great and powerful that it catches others in a moment, and thousands are drawn towards them, and half the world think as they do. Great prophets of the world had the most wonderful control of the Prana, which gave them tremendous will-power; they had brought their Prana to the highest state of motion, and this is what gave them power to sway the world. All manifestations of power arise from this control. Men may not know the secret, but this is the one explanation. Sometimes in your own body the supply of Prana gravitates more or less to one part; the balance is disturbed, and when the balance of Prana is disturbed, what we call disease is produced. To take away the superfluous Prana, or to supply the Prana that is wanting, will be curing the disease. That again is Pranayama — to learn when there is more or less Prana in one part of the body than there should be. The feelings will become so subtle that the mind will feel that there is less Prana in the toe or the finger than there should be, and will possess the power to supply it. These are among the various functions of Pranayama. They have to be learned slowly and gradually, and as you see, the whole scope of Raja-Yoga is really to teach the control and direction in different planes of the Prana. When a man has concentrated his energies, he masters the Prana that is in his body. When a man is meditating, he is also concentrating the Prana.

Think of the universe as an ocean of ether, consisting of layer after layer of varying degrees of vibration under the action of Prana; away from the centre the vibrations are less, nearer to it they become quicker and quicker; one order of vibration makes one plane. Then suppose these ranges of vibrations are cut into planes, so many millions of miles one set of vibration, and then so many millions of miles another still higher set of vibration, and so on. It is, therefore, probable, that those who live on the plane of a certain state of vibration will have the power of recognising one another, but will not recognise those above them. Yet, just as by the telescope and the microscope we can increase the scope of our vision, similarly we can by Yoga bring ourselves to the state of vibration of another plane, and thus enable ourselves to see what is going on there. Suppose this room is full of beings whom we do not see. They represent Prana in a certain state of vibration while we represent another. Suppose they represent a quick one, and we the opposite. Prana is the material of which the: are composed, as well as we. All are parts of the same ocean of

Prana, they differ only in their rate of vibration. If I can bring myself to the quick vibration, this plane will immediately change for me: I shall not see you any more; you vanish and they appear. Some of you, perhaps, know this to be true. All this bringing of the mind into a higher state of vibration is included in one word in Yoga — Samadhi. All these states of higher vibration, superconscious vibrations of the mind, are grouped in that one word, Samadhi, and the lower states of Samadhi give us visions of these beings. The highest grade of Samadhi is when we see the real thing, when we see the material out of which the whole of these grades of beings are composed, and that one lump of clay being known, we know all the clay in the universe.

Thus we see that Pranayama includes all that is true of spiritualism even. Similarly, you will find that wherever any sect or body of people is trying to search out anything occult and mystical, or hidden, what they are doing is really this Yoga, this attempt to control the Prana. You will find that wherever there is any extraordinary display of power, it is the manifestation of this Prana. Even the physical sciences can be included in Pranayama. What moves the steam engine? Prana, acting through the steam. What are all these phenomena of electricity and so forth but Prana? What is physical science? The science of Pranayama, by external means. Prana, manifesting itself as mental power, can only be controlled by mental means. That part of Pranayama which attempts to control the physical manifestations of the Prana by physical means is called physical science, and that part which tries to control the manifestations of the Prana as mental force by mental means is called Raja-Yoga....

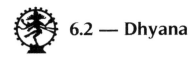# 6.2 — Dhyana

Swami Vivekananda

...In order to reach the superconscious state in a scientific manner it is necessary to pass through the various steps of Raja-Yoga I have been teaching. [W]e now come to Dhyana, meditation. When the mind has been trained to remain fixed on a certain internal or external location, there comes to it the power of flowing in an unbroken current, as it were, towards that point. This state is called Dhyana. When one has so intensified the power of Dhyana as to be able to reject the external part of perception and remain meditating only on the internal part, the meaning, that state is called Samadhi. The three — Dharana, Dhyana, and Samadhi — together, are called Samyama. That is, if the mind can first concentrate upon an object, and then is able to continue in that concentration for a length of time, and then, by continued concentration, to dwell only on the internal part of the perception of which the object was the effect, everything comes under the control of such a mind.

This meditative state is the highest state of existence. So long as there is desire, no real happiness can come. It is only the contemplative, witness-like study of objects that brings to us real enjoyment and happiness. The animal has its happiness in the senses, the man in his intellect, and the god in spiritual contemplation. It is only to the soul that has attained to this contemplative state that the world really becomes beautiful. To him who desires nothing, and does not mix himself up with them, the manifold changes of nature are one panorama of beauty and sublimity.

These ideas have to be understood in Dhyana, or meditation. We hear a sound. First, there is the external vibration; second, the nerve motion that carries it to the mind; third, the reaction from the mind, along with which flashes the knowledge of the object which was the external cause of these different changes from the ethereal vibrations to the mental reactions. These three are called in Yoga, Shabda (sound), Artha (meaning), and Jnâna (knowledge). In the language of physics and physiology they are called the ethereal vibration, the motion in the nerve and brain, and the mental reaction. Now these, though distinct processes, have become mixed up in such a fashion as to become quite indistinct. In fact, we cannot now perceive any of these, we only perceive their combined effect, what we

Swami Vivekananda. "Raja Yoga." *The Four Yogas.* New York: SophiaOmni, 2017.

call the external object. Every act of perception includes these three, and there is no reason why we should not be able to distinguish them.

When, by the previous preparations, it becomes strong and controlled, and has the power of finer perception, the mind should be employed in meditation. This meditation must begin with gross objects and slowly rise to finer and finer, until it becomes objectless. The mind should first be employed in perceiving the external causes of sensations, then the internal motions, and then its own reaction. When it has succeeded in perceiving the external causes of sensations by themselves, the mind will acquire the power of perceiving all fine material existences, all fine bodies and forms. When it can succeed in perceiving the motions inside by themselves, it will gain the control of all mental waves, in itself or in others, even before they have translated themselves into physical energy; and when he will be able to perceive the mental reaction by itself, the Yogi will acquire the knowledge of everything, as every sensible object, and every thought is the result of this reaction. Then will he have seen the very foundations of his mind, and it will be under his perfect control. Different powers will come to the Yogi, and if he yields to the temptations of any one of these, the road to his further progress will be barred. Such is the evil of running after enjoyments. But if he is strong enough to reject even these miraculous powers, he will attain to the goal of Yoga, the complete suppression of the waves in the ocean of the mind. Then the glory of the soul, undisturbed by the distractions of the mind, or motions of the body, will shine in its full effulgence; and the Yogi will find himself as he is and as he always was, the essence of knowledge, the immortal, the all-pervading.

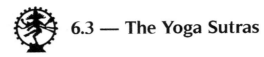# 6.3 — The Yoga Sutras

Patanjali

Part One
Samadhi (Samadhi Pada)

The first part of the Yoga Sutras focuses on samadhi or absorption. The aim of samadhi, as we'll see, is to allow the meditator to attain a state of calmness of mind in which the Self can be manifested.

What is Yoga?

The definition of yoga is given along with two options for consciousness.

¹ Now we come to instruction in yoga.

² Yoga is the stilling (*nirodha*) of the fluctuations (*vritti*) of consciousness (*citta*).

³ When this is accomplished, then the seer abides in his true nature.

⁴ Otherwise the seer identifies with the fluctuations of consciousness.

On the Fluctuations of Consciousness

The five types of fluctuations of consciousness are treated.

⁵ There are five fluctuations of consciousness, and these are either afflictive (*klista*) or non-afflictive (*aklista*).

⁶ These are right knowledge, error, conceptualization, sleep, and memory.

⁷ Right knowledge arises from direct perception, inference, and from the words of others.

⁸ Error is false knowledge and is not based upon the reality of what is.

⁹ Conceptualization is derived from words, not from contact with real objects.

Yoga Sutras. Trans. Michael S. Russo

[10] Sleep is a state of mind devoid of any content.

[11] Memory is the recollection of sense impressions that one has experienced.

Controlling the Fluctuations of Consciousness

This section describes how the fluctuations of consciousness can be controlled through practice and non-attachment.

[12] Practice and non-attachment are required to still the fluctuations of consciousness.

[13] Practice is the sustained effort to still these fluctuations.

[14] Practice becomes well rooted when it is cultivated skillfully over a long period of time.

[15] Non-attachment is achieved when the mind attains a state of desirelessness with regard to sense objects.

[16] When the highest level of non-attachment has been achieved, the Spirit (*purusha*) can be seen as distinct from the qualities of material nature (*gunas*).

On The Two Forms of Samadhi

Patanjali now goes on to describe the two types of samadhi: (1) A conscious form of samadhi uses ordinary mental processes to still the mind; (2) on a deeper level, all thought is completely stilled so that only past impressions remain.

[17] Conscious *samadhi* [*samprajnata samadhi*] can result from the mental processes of analysis, reflection, bliss, or ego consciousness.

[18] Beyond this is the state of nonconscious *samadhi* [*asamprajnata samadhi*] achieved by the practice of constant concentration in which only subtle impressions remain.

[19] For those freed of bodies, if there remains enmeshment in material nature, this becomes the cause of rebirth.

[20] For all others, the path to realization is achieved though faith, energy, mindfulness, and wisdom.

[21] For those who apply themselves ardently, this state is readily realizable.

[22] How realizable it is depends upon whether one's practice is mild, moderate, or intense.

Devotion to the Lord

Samadhi can also be achieved through the practice of devotion to the Ishvara (creative source or deity). Also briefly discussed in this section of the text is the sacred syllable OM (or AUM), which expresses ultimate reality.

[23] The state of *samadhi* can also come from devotion to the Lord (*Ishvara*).

[24] The Lord is a special form of spirit (*purusha*) unaffected by the forces of corruption, action (*karma*), the fruits of action, or the latent impressions that cause those actions.

[25] In the Lord the seed of omniscience has reached its highest and unsurpassed form.

[26] Unconstrained by time, it is by him that even the most ancient teachers were taught.

[27] The word that represents him is the sacred syllable OM.

[28] Repeating this syllable reveals its meaning.

[29] From the remembrance of OM comes the realization of the Self and the removal of obstacles to that realization.

Overcoming the Obstacles to Concentration

There are several causes of the mind's distraction. In order to overcome these distractions, the practice of single-pointed concentration is recommended.

[30] There are nine kinds of distraction that are obstacles to concentration. These are sickness, apathy, doubt, carelessness, laziness, dissipation, false views, failure to attain proficiency in yoga, and unsteadiness.

[31] From these obstacles there also arises suffering, frustration, restlessness, and irregularities in breathing.

[32] The way to prevent these obstacles from arising is to engage in the practice of training the mind to concentrate on a single object.

Attaining Calmness of Mind

Practices are offered which will lead to calmness of mind. Treated first are habits of behavior aimed at transforming one's relationship to others. The remaining practices are focused on breath-control (pranayama) and other activities aimed at concentrating the mind on particular objects.

[33] Calmness of mind is attained by cultivating the habits of friendliness towards those who are happy, compassion towards in sorrow, goodwill towards the virtuous, equanimity towards those we perceive as wicked.

[34] Or through the controlled expulsion and retention of the breath.

[35] Or by focusing on some object of perception.

[36] Or by fixing the mind on some internal luminous state that is free of sorrow.

[37] Or by focusing on things that are free from attachment.

[38] Or by reflecting on insights attained through the dream state in sleep.

[39] Or through meditative absorption on any desired object.

[40] Through such practices the mind can concentrate on any object from the infinitesimally small to the incredibly vast.

Absorption "with Seed"

The state of complete absorption (samapattih or samadhi), in which thought is completely unified with specific objects of concentration, is discussed. These objects can be gross (i.e., external sense objects) or subtle (i.e., internal). They can be grasped either through conceptualization (naming, identifying, and knowing) or without conceptualization. This is called absorption "with seed" because it provides the foundation for future thoughts.

[41] When the movements of thought have subsided, the mind becomes like a transparent jewel and thus can take on the qualities of whatever object it concentrates on, whether that object is the subject itself, the act of observing, or the object observed. This state is known as complete absorption (*samapattih*).

[42] When the mind achieves a state of absorption with conceptualization (*savitarka-samapattih*) this state is accompanied by the naming of the object, the identification of the object, and knowledge of the object.

[43] When the mind achieves a state of absorption without conceptualization (*nirvitarka-samapattih*) this state is unaccompanied by the naming of the object, the meaning of the object, and knowledge of the object.

[44] When the object of absorption is a subtle object, two kinds of absorption, known as absorption with subtle conceptualization (*savichara-samapattih*) and absorption without subtle conceptualization (*nirvichara-samapattih*) may be distinguished in the same manner.

[45] Subtle objects can be traced back to their source in primordial nature (*prakriti*).

[46] These four types of absorption [i.e., with conceptualization, without conceptualization, with subtle conceptualization, without subtle conceptualization] are said to be "with seed" (*sabijah*).

Absorption "without Seed"

Absorption "without seed" is a state of pure absorption in which the meditator gains direct knowledge of the object of concentration. Because this knowledge is direct, rather than being conceptual, no new thoughts are generated.

[47] Upon attaining the clarity of absorption without subtle conceptualization, the nature of the Self becomes manifested.

[48] The knowledge that arises from that state is truth-bearing.

[49] This knowledge is different knowledge arising from teaching or through inference, because it is direct knowledge.

[50] This type of knowledge creates impressions (*samskarah*) that inhibit the formation of other kinds of impressions.

[51] When the impressions made by this kind of truth-bearing knowledge recede along with other impressions, then one enters into a state of absorption that is said to be "without seed" (*nirbijah*).

Part Two
Practices (Sadhana Pada)

The word "sadhana" means "practice" or "discipline." This refers specifically to those yogic practices that allow the meditator to attain a state of Self-realization. In this part of the text we get Patanjali's famous description of the "eight limbs of yoga" which are presented like a ladder, enabling the meditator ultimately to achieve liberation.

The Purpose of Yogic Practice

The aim of yoga is to remove those mental afflictions that lead to suffering and allow one to attain the state of samadhi.

[1] Active yoga has three components: austerity (*tapas*), self-study (*svadhyaya*), and devotion to the Lord (*ishvara*).

[2] Its purpose is to remove afflictions of the mind (*kleshas*) and to attain a state of perfect concentration (*samadhi*).

The Five Causes and Overcoming of Affliction

The five causes of the afflictions are discussed.

[3] There are five causes of affliction: ignorance (*avidya*), egoism (*asmita*), attachment (*raja*), aversion (*devesa*), and clinging to life (*abhinivesa*).

[4] Ignorance is the root of all the other afflictions, whether they are dormant, weak, intermittent, or active.

[5] Ignorance is regarding the transient as eternal, the impure as pure, the sorrowful for that which brings happiness, and that which is not the Self as the Self.

[6] Egoism (*asmita* = I-ness) is the mistake of identifying pure consciousness with the processes of sense perception.

[7] Attachment (*ragah*) follows from the experience of the pleasurable.

[8] Aversion (*dvesah*) follows from the experience of the painful.

[9] Clinging to life is a natural tendency that affects even the wise.

[10] In their subtle form, these afflictions can be overcome when they are traced back to their source.

[11] The movements of the mind [caused by these afflictions] can be subdued through meditation (*dhyana*).

The Nature and Consequences of Karma

The afflictions create subtle impressions (samskara) that are the cause of suffering in this life and in future lives.

[12] The storehouse of *karma* has its roots in the afflictions and these will be realized in the present or in some future life.

[13] So long as these roots exist, they will bear fruit in the form of a rebirth, a life, and the experiences of that life.

[14] Such a life will be characterized by pleasure or pain in proportion to the good or bad actions that one performs.

[15] For the wise, all life is characterized by suffering, because even pleasurable experiences are subject to change, lead to future distress, and create subtle [habit-forming] impressions (*samskara*).

[16] But that suffering which is to come can be avoided.

The Seer and the Seen

The ultimate cause of the afflictions that lead to suffering is the identification of consciousness (the seer, Purusha) with material reality (prakriti).

[17] The cause of this suffering is the identification of the seer (*Purusha*) with the seen (*prakriti*).

[18] The seen is comprised of the three fundamental qualities of nature (*gunas*): illumination (*sattva*), activity (*rajas*), and inertia (*tamas*). It consists of the senses and the material elements and exists to provide sense experience or liberation [to *purusha*].

[19] The three qualities of nature are manifested as undifferentiated or differentiated, indistinctive or distinctive.

[20] The seer is nothing but the power of seeing itself, which, through pure consciousness, appears to operate through the power of the mind.

[21] The seen exists exclusively for the sake of the seer.

[22] Although the seen ceases to exist for he who has attained liberation, it continues to exist as a common reality for everyone else.

[23] The union of the seer with the seen is the necessary means whereby the nature and powers of both can be known.

[24] The false identification of the seer with the seen is caused by ignorance (*avidya*).

[25] When this ignorance has been destroyed, this false identification ceases. This leads to a state of liberation for the seer.

[26] Focused discriminative knowledge (*viveka-khyatih*) is the means whereby ignorance is destroyed.

[27] Seven kinds of ultimate wisdom (*prajna*) come to one who has attained this kind of discriminative knowledge.

The Eight Limbs of Yoga

The eight limbs of yoga are introduced as the means of revealing the true nature of the Self, and hence of eradicating suffering.

[28] Through the practice of the eight limbs of yoga, all impurities are removed. Then the light of understanding can shine forth by focused discriminative knowledge.

[29] The eight limbs of yoga are the codes of moral restraint (*yamas*), the various observances (*niyamas*), posture (*asana*), breath control (*pranayama*), withdrawal of the mind from sense objects (*pratyahara*), concentration (*dharana*), meditation (*dhyana*), and complete absorption (*samadhi*).

The Moral Restraints and Personal Observances

The first two (external) limbs of yoga involve moral restraint and personal observances.

[30] The Moral restraints (*yamas*) consist of non-violence (ahimsa), truthfulness (*satya*), not stealing (*asteya*), celibacy (*brahmacharya*), and non-greed (*aparigraha*).

[31] These moral restraints are universal and are not restricted by any considerations of one's class, place, time, or circumstance.

[32] The observances (*niyamas*) consist of purity (*saucha*), contentment (*santosha*), discipline (*tapas*), self (*svadhyaya*), and devotion to God (*ishvara-pranidhana*).

[33] Thoughts that run contrary to the restraints and observances (i.e., unwholesome thoughts) can be countered by cultivating opposing thoughts (i.e., wholesome thoughts).

[34] Unwholesome thoughts, such as wanting to harm someone, may be acted upon by ourselves or we may cause or condone them in others; they may arise from anger, greed, or delusion; they can be mild, moderate, or intense in nature. One must always remind oneself that they are an endless source of misery and ignorance. This is why it is important to cultivate counteracting thoughts.

The Benefits of the Moral Restraints

Patanjali discusses the various benefits involved in practicing the moral restraints.

[35] When one becomes firmly established in non-violence, others who enter one's presence will abandon their feelings of hostility.

[36] When one becomes firmly established in truthfulness, all actions and their results become grounded in the truth.

[37] When ones becomes firmly established in non-stealing, all wealth comes.

[38] When one becomes firmly established in celibacy, vitality is gained.

[39] When one becomes firmly established in non-greed, an insight into the nature of rebirth is revealed.

The Benefits of the Personal Observances

The various benefits involved in following the personal observances are also discussed.

[40] With purity, one becomes disinterested in one's own body and disinclined towards physical contact with others.

[41] With purity also comes clarity, cheerfulness, concentration, control over the senses, and the capacity for Self-realization.

[42] With contentment comes supreme joy.

[43] With discipline comes the destruction of impurities and the perfection of the body and its senses.

[44] With study comes contact with one's personal deity (*ista-devata*).

[45] With devotion to God comes the attainment of s*amadhi*.

Posture

A simple definition of proper posture is described to aid in meditation.

[46] Meditation posture (*asana*) should be steady and comfortable.

[47] This occurs by the relaxation of effort and by meditating on the infinite within.

[48] Then one is no longer troubled by dualities.

Breath Control

The regulation of prana (bodily energy) through breath control is now treated.

[49] With relaxed posture being achieved, the flow of inhalation and exhalation should be regulated. This is called breath control (*pranayama*).

[50] The fluctuations of the breath manifest themselves in exhalation, inhalation, and retention. These can be regulated in terms of duration, number, and place of focus and are either long or short.

[51] A fourth type of breath control goes beyond the range of exhalation and inhalation.

[52] Then the veil covering the inner light is removed.

[53] And the mind becomes fit for concentration (*dharana*).

Withdrawal of the Senses

Withdrawal of the senses leads the meditator from the external world to the internal world.

[54] When consciousness is uncoupled from sense objects, the senses follow suit, withdrawing themselves from their objects, and thus begin to imitate consciousness. This is known as withdrawal of the senses (*pratyahara*).

[55] Then the supreme mastery over the senses occurs.

Part Three
Accomplishments (Vibhuti Pada)

The third part of the Yoga Sutras focuses on the vibhuti, which are the accomplishments that come as yoga practice progresses. The text also describes supernormal powers (siddhis) that can be achieved when one masters the practices of concentration, meditation, and absorption. Combined, these practices are referred to as "perfect discipline" (samyama). This part of the text goes on to point out the dangers of the supernormal powers, which can actually distract one from the goal of liberation and which therefore should be treated with caution.

Concentration, Meditation, and Absorption

The discussion commences with an all-too-brief treatment of the last three internal limbs of yoga.

[1] Concentration (*dharana*) is the fixing of consciousness on one object.

[2] In meditation (*dhyana*) a steady and continuous flow of awareness is directed towards that object.

[3] When only the essential nature of the object shines forth, without form, complete absorption (*samadhi*) has occurred.

[4] The practice of these three (concentration, meditation, and absorption) together constitute perfect discipline (*samyama*).

[5] From mastery of perfect discipline comes the light of wisdom (*prajna*).

[6] Perfect discipline is to be accomplished in stages.

[7] In contrast with the preceding five limbs, these three limbs (concentration, meditation, and absorption) are more internal.

[8] But even these three limbs are external when compared to absorption without seed.

Part Four
Liberation (Kaivalya Pada)

Attaining Liberation

The Sanskrit term "kaivalya" specifically means "isolation" or "detachment" and represents the goal of yoga practice—the isolation of purusha from prakriti that leads to liberation (moksha). The term therefore is often used synonymously with moksha.

[29] One who is completely disinterested upon attaining the highest state imaginable, maintaining supreme discrimination in all circumstances, enters the final stage of absorption, called the cloud of dharma (*dharma-megha*) absorption.

[30] From that state of absorption, all afflictions and *karmas* cease.

[31] When the veils of the impurities are removed, the infinity of knowl-

edge is attained, and what remains to be known is almost nothing.

[32] Then the sequence of mutations of the qualities of nature (*gunas*) cease, since they have fulfilled their purpose.

[33] This sequence is an uninterrupted succession taking place every moment, but is only recognized at the end of their mutations.

[34] Liberation (*kaivalya*) comes when the qualities of nature (*gunas*) resolve themselves into their original primal state (*prakriti*), since they have no further purpose to serve the Spirit (*purusha*). Then the Sprit shines forth in its own true nature.

PRACTICE

Pranayama

As we've seen, the Sanskrit term "pranayama" literally means to "regulate" or "lengthen" (*ayama*) the breath (*prana*). But the world "*prana*" actually means something more than just breath in yogic philosophy: it is the "life force"; it's that which gives energy, vitality, and harmony to our lives.

While it's true that our emotional states tend to affect our breathing patterns—for example, when we're afraid or anxious, our breaths tend to be shallow and rapid—the opposite has also been found to be true: by skillfully regulating our breathing patterns, we can, in fact, transform our emotional states.

Practice 1: Noticing the Breath

Before trying to regulate your breathing patterns, we're going to return to a practice that we tried in Chapter 2 of this text—simply noticing the breath. Here's how we do it:

1. Begin by sitting comfortably in a chair with your hands on your lap and just take notice of your breath. Is your breath shallow or deep, smooth or choppy? Are you breathing from your nose or from your mouth?
2. Next, put your hand on your belly. As you breathe in, note what's happening with your stomach, Is it expanding, contracting, or not moving much at all?
3. Now, just spend a minute or two following the flow of your breath as you breathe in and out. You don't need to alter your breathing patters in any way; just allow your breath to flow in and out naturally. After simply observing your breath in this way, do you notice any changes to the way you are breathing?

What you just did in a few minutes is to become aware of an activity that most of us tend to do automatically and without much thought at all. After all, you've been breathing since the moment you were born: if you weren't you wouldn't be reading this right now.

Breathing, in other words, is something we just tend to do. But pranayama—yogic breathing—is something a bit different from this: it involves the intentional act of regulating the breath to achieve physical and mental well-being.

Practice 2: Abdominal Breathing

Most adults tend to breathe from the chest and our breathing patterns, therefore, tend to be quite shallow. Typically, with each in-breath, our stomachs contract, and, with each out-breath, our stomachs expand. The problem with this sort of breathing is that it can signal to the brain that you are anxious, and this is a recipe for a stressed-out life.

Compare the way we adults typically breathe with the way a baby breathes. If you've ever seen a baby lying in a crib, you've undoubtedly observed that he tends to take full deep, breaths. With each in-breath, the baby's stomach expands and with each out-breath, his stomach contracts. A baby knows intuitively how to breathe in such a way as to maximize oxygen flow to the lungs. This, in fact, is the way that nature intended all of us to breathe.

This natural way of breathing is known as abdominal or yogic breathing and it's something that we can all learn again, no matter how old we are. The benefits of this sort of breathing are that it tends to help create a sense of calm and centeredness and can serve to mitigate intense emotional states.

Here's how to do it:

1. Sit comfortably on a chair or meditation cushion with your spine straight and your eyes shut.
2. Begin breathing deeply in through your nose. As you breathe in, you should feel your stomach expand and your chest rise. Inhale slowly, filling your lungs with as much oxygen as possible.
3. Now exhale slowly. You should experience your stomach contracting and your chest dropping. As you exhale, try to expel as much oxygen as you can from your lungs without causing any discomfort or strain.
4. Try to hold each in- and out breath for a count of 5, 8, or 10 seconds—whatever you can manage comfortably without strain.
5. Try doing 5-10 rounds of this kind of deep breathing.

After you're finished doing several rounds of this type of breathing, take stock of how you are feeling. Normally, deep abdominal breathing should make you feel calmer and more relaxed—the exact opposite of how you would feel if your breath was more rapid and shallow.

Practice 3: Alternate Nostril Breathing (Nadi Shodhana)

Alternate Nostril Breathing has been found to be a wonderful technique for calming the nervous system and concentrating the mind. The name for this form of *pranayama* comes from the fact that when practicing this type of breathing, we alternate between the two nostrils, breathing from only one nostril at a time. This practice may seem a bit strange at first, but once you get the practice of it, it becomes much easier.

Begin by sitting comfortably with your left hand on your left knee and your eyes closed. Bring your right hand to your face.

1. Press your right thumb down on your right nostril and exhale through your left nostril.
2. Inhale through the left nostril, and then press it closed with your right ring finger.
3. Release the thumb from your right nostril and exhale through the right nostril.
4. Inhale through the right nostril, and then press it closed with your thumb.
5. This completes one full round of alternate nostril breathing. Continue with about 5-10 more rounds of this type of breathing.
6. Sit quietly for a few moments after you've finished or begin meditation.

Please note that this practice should not be attempted if you have a cold or your nasal passages are blocked for some reason. Also, if you start to feel yourself getting lightheaded while doing this practice, you should stop immediately.

Because of the calming effect that alternate nostril breathing has, this is a wonderful practice to try during times when you're feeling stressed or need to clear your mind—before an exam, for example. It can also be of help if you have difficulty falling asleep at night.

7
The *Bhagavad Gita*:
A Synthesis of Hindu Thought

Contained within the text of the massive Hindu epic *The Mahabharata* is the 700-verse *Bhagavad Gita*—literally, "The Song of the Lord." Authorship of the text, like that of the *Mahabharata* itself, is ascribed to the sage Vyasa, although most scholars today tend to doubt that the *Gita* is the work of a single individual. While the date of composition of the *Gita* is difficult to determine, it is usually dated somewhere between the 5th and 2nd centuries BCE. Like most Hindu texts, the *Gita* was probably the result of centuries of oral tradition, in which a foundational text was elaborated and expanded upon until it more or less achieved its present form.

The *Gita* has an exalted status among Hindus and is most certainly the most well-known and influential Hindu text for non-Hindus. It is considered one of the world's great spiritual classics—as important a work in its own right as the *Bible*, the *Koran*, the texts of the Pali Cannon, or the *Tao Te Ching*. One significant reason for the popularity of the text is undoubtedly the universality of its message, which has helped it to resonate with wisdom-seekers from across religious traditions.

The universality of the text might have something to do with the fact that the *Gita* is eclectic enough to bear almost any interpretation. Numerous commentaries on the *Gita* have been written by teachers from widely divergent schools of thought, and interpretations of the meaning of the text often differ profoundly. The virtue, then, of the *Gita* lies in its ability to encompass a wide variety of different spiritual traditions and practices as though these were simply alternative paths on the same journey to liberation. To put it simply, there is something in the text to appeal to almost everyone.

But this is also the work's liability. Those seeking a consistent or unified philosophical message are bound to be sorely disappointed. And most attempts by commentators to impose some kind of doctrinal structure upon the text have, quite frankly, failed miserably. As Jeaneane Fowler observes, "those who find the *Gita* favors one or another path to liberation will too readily find that favored path contradicted by another in the text."[1]

Although the text expresses a decidedly devotional form of Hinduism—one that emphasizes devotion to Krishna—the *Gita* actually represents a synthesis of all Hindu thought, since each of the four yogic paths that we have examined is treated in the work to one degree or another. As we've seen, some of these yogic paths contradict one another both in their teachings as well as in their recommended practices. The *Gita*, however, sweeps aside these contradictions in its attempt at inclusivity and universality.

The Setting of the Text

In order to fully understand what is going on in the *Bhagavad Gita*, a bit of background is definitely helpful. The *Mahabharata* tells the story of the conflict between two branches of the same family—the Kuravas and the Pandavas—to determine who will rule India. According to this tale, the leader of the Pandavas, Yudhishthira, lost his kingdom for thirteen years in a game of dice and he and his family were forced into exile during that period. When the period of exile was completed, the Pandavas return to reclaim their kingdom, but the Kuravas refuse to honor their agreement. All attempts at reconciliation fail and the two sides prepare for war.

The *Bhagavad Gita* opens on the eve of battle between the Pandavas and the Kuravas. Arjuna, one of the Pandavas, is riding in his chariot and is suddenly filled with despondency at the thought of having to kill his relatives and friends. At the opening of the *Gita*, Arjuna sits down on the battlefield and simply refuses to fight (1.20-2.9).

With Arjuna during this conflict is Krishna, his charioteer. Throughout the *Gita*, Krishna serves as Arjuna's friend and confidant, so it's not surprising that Arjuna would turn to him for guidance. What is surprising is Krishna's response to Arjuna's dilemma (2.10-38). Given that *ahimsa* (non-injury or non-violence) is a central part of Hindu ethics, we would naturally expect Krishna to support Arjuna's decision not to go to war against the Kurvas. In fact, Krishna rebukes Arjuna for his "unmanliness" and urges him to fight.

What makes this counsel even more surprising is that eventually in the text Krishna will reveal himself to be the Lord of the Universe—an incarnation of the god Vishnu. So what we essentially have in the *Gita* is a divine being advising one of his devotees to slaughter his enemies for the sake of righteousness (*dharma*). This also seems to contradict other advice that Krishna gives Arjuna throughout the text, when he instructs him to see all beings as one, to treat them with compassion, and avoid harming anyone.

So what are we to make of Krishna's exhortation to warfare in the text?

The simple answer is the one that Krishna states directly in the second chapter of the work: liberation comes from following one's *dharma*—one's duty as a member of a particular caste. Arjuna is a member of the warrior caste, so his duty is to fight when called to do so, particularly when the cause is a righteous one (2.31-38). But this answer still doesn't resolve the difficulties involved in having Krishna—the ever compassionate Lord of the Universe—counsel his devotee to slaughter his enemies in battle.

One way to get around this difficulty is to do what Swami Vivekanada did and interpret the idea of the battle in the text as allegorical. The battle in this interpretation, therefore, is the battle waged in Arjuna's soul between his higher Self and his lower inclinations.[2] This is essentially the approach that Eknath Easwaran also takes in his wonderful translation of the *Gita*. The struggle presented in the *Gita*, Easwaran writes, is the struggle for self-mastery that all of us face. It is a metaphor for "the perennial war between the forces of light and the forces of darkness in every human heart."[3] Interpreted this way, the opening of the *Gita* makes much more sense and is far more consistent with the teachings of the rest of the text.

The *Gita* and the Four Yogic Paths

The question that begins the *Bhagavad Gita* is what is the right way for a warrior like Arjuna to behave in light of the approaching battle with his relatives. But we've seen that the battle in question can be metaphorically understood as the inner struggle for liberation. And so, the central question of the text can be understood more broadly as, what is the right way of life for *anyone* seeking liberation. Since different people have different temperaments, a variety of paths will have to be introduced.

Like the *Upanishads*, the *Gita* presents the view that *Atman* is identical to Brahman and suggests that the path of knowledge (*Jnana Yoga*) is a suitable one for liberation. In this sense, the text can be seen as compatible with Vedantic philosophy. But this path is also regarded as a difficult one for the vast majority of human beings, especially for someone like Arjuna, who clearly does not possess a philosophical temperament. The path of meditation (*Raja Yoga*) is also presented as a viable option, though once again, not necessarily for one who has difficulties concentrating his mind. For Arjuna, two preferable paths remain—the path of selfless action (*Karma Yoga*) and the path of devotion (*Bhakti Yoga*). Either of these,

Krishna tells Arjuna, will lead him to liberation. We should keep in mind, however, that Krishna is specifically advising a man of the warrior caste—someone with an active temperament. His advice presumably would not be the same for someone with a philosophical or contemplative bent.

The key, I believe, to understanding the *Gita* lies in the famous quote from Chapter 4, Verse 11: "Whatever way people try to reach Me, I accept them; whatever path they may travel, it eventually leads to Me." Although the emphasis in the text may be devotional—focused on the divinity of Krisha—there clearly is a recognition that any of the four yogic paths will lead one to liberation.

 Selection — The Bhagavad Gita

NOTES

1. Jeaneane Fowler. *The Bhagavad Gita: A Text and Commentary for Students* (Eastbourne, GB: Sussex Academic Press, 2012): xxvii.
2. Swami Vivekananda. "Thoughts on the Gita." *Complete Works*. Vol. 4: Lectures and Discourses.
3. *The Bhagavad Gita*. Trans. Eknath Easwarn (Tomales, CA: Nilgiri Press, 2007): 21.

SOURCES

THE *BHAGAVAD GITA*

This heavily edited translation of the Bhagavad Gita *focuses mainly on the first two-thirds of the text (Chapters 1-12). This is where the reader will encounter both the most popular sections of the work as well as those passages which deal specifically with the four yogic paths. You'll notice that I've opted to edit the text in such a way as to cluster texts dealing with specific yogic paths together to try to make the meaning of these texts clearer to the reader. It should also be noted that the original Sanskrit version of the* Gita *was composed in verses of mainly 32 meters. I've opted for a prose translation, recognizing that this choice necessarily sacrifices much of the majestic poetry of the text. Those who would like to read a more traditional version of this text are encouraged to read the highly regarded version by Eknath Easwaran (Nilgiri Press, 2007), which combines clarity with grace of expression.*

OPENING OF THE TEXT

Arjuna's Dilemma [1.20-40, 44-47]

Arjuna beheld the sons of Dhritarashtra, assembled on the battlefield, ready to fight. Raising his bow, he said to his charioteer, "Krishna, move my chariot between the two armies, so that I can see those who are fighting on my side and those who are fighting against me."

Driving his shining chariot between the two armies and facing those kings, Krishna said "Arjuna, behold the members of the Kuru family assembled here."

Arjuna saw before him fathers, grandfathers, uncles, cousins, sons, grandsons, teachers, friends, fathers-in-law, and comrades arrayed in both armies.

Gazing at them there, his heart was filled with great sorrow and he said, "Krishna, when I see my own kinsmen gathered here lusting for battle, my limbs are weakened and my mouth goes dry; my body shakes and my hair

---

Bhagavad Gita. Trans. Michael S. Russo

stands on end; my bow is slipping from my hand and my skin is burning; I can't stand still, for my mind is in turmoil.

I see bad omens, Krishna, for what good can come from slaughtering my own kinsmen on the battlefield? I don't seek victory, or kingdoms, or pleasures. For what use are power, or enjoyments, or even life itself, when those for whom I desire these things are now ready to abandon their lives and riches in battle....Krishna, what happiness can come from killing these sons of Dhritarashtra? In killing these desperate men, aren't we in fact committing sin? I wouldn't want to kill them, even to become the ruler of the [entire universe], much less to rule over this world. It doesn't matter if I am killed.

Even if the minds of these men are overcome by greed and they are blind to the evil that they cause by destroying their family and betraying their friends, how can we, who clearly see the evil involved in destroying family, not refrain from committing such sin?

When the family is destroyed, family traditions and codes of moral conduct are destroyed with it....And we have been told, Krishna, that they are forever lost who allow such family traditions to be lost. What a great sin, then, I commit, if I am willing to kill my own kinsmen for the pleasures of a kingdom. It would be better for my own welfare if I allowed them to kill me in battle while I am unresisting and unarmed."

Having said this, Arjuna cast his bow and arrows onto the battlefield. He sat down on the seat of his chariot, his mind overcome by sorrow.

Krishna Urges Arjuna to Fight [2.1-7, 9]

Seeing Arjuna, whose eyes were sorrowful and whose mind was depressed, Krishna spoke these words: "Why has this dejection come over you at such a perilous time? It is not worthy of a noble mind. It will not lead you to heaven and will only bring you infamy. Such unmanliness is unworthy of you, so do not give into it. Banish this petty weakness from your heart and arise for battle, Arjuna!"

Arjuna replied, "Krishna, how can I attack men like Bhisma and Drona who are worthy of my respect? It would be far better for me to live in this world as a beggar than to slay these noble men. If I killed them, the wealth and pleasures that I would enjoy would be stained by their blood.

And I don't know which would be worse—to win this battle or to lose it. I should not even wish to live if I had to kill these men standing in front of us.

My heart is overcome by pity and my mind is confused about where my duty (*dharma*) lies. Krishna, I ask you to tell me frankly what the right thing to do is. I am your pupil. Please instruct me!"...

After speaking like this to Krishna, Arjuna said, "O Krishna, I will not fight!" and was silent.

Fulfilling One's Dharma [2.10, 31-38]

Krishna, smiling, spoke the following words to the distressed Arjuna as they stood in the midst of the two armies...: "Regarding your duty (*dharma*) as a warrior, you should not falter. There is no higher good for a warrior than a battle fought for the sake of duty. Fortunate indeed are warriors who have a war like this thrust upon them by chance. It is like an open door to heaven.

But if you do not fight this battle, then you will fail in your duty, incur sin, and lose your reputation as a warrior. People will talk of your infamy forever. And for one who has experienced honor, infamy is worse than death. These great warriors will think that you have left the battlefield on account of fear, and will treat you as an object of derision. Your enemies will speak of you with insulting words, mocking your courage. Could anything be worse for you than that?

If you are killed, you will win heaven; if you triumph you will enjoy the earthly kingdom. Therefore, get up with determination and fight, Arjuna! With no thought to joy or sorrow, loss or gain, victory or defeat, prepare to do your duty and fight. By fulfilling your duty in this way, you will not incur sin."

THE PATH OF SELF-KNOWLEDGE

The Nature of the Self [2.11-13, 16-27]

Krishna said, "Although you mean well, you grieve for those for whom no grief is due. The wise grieve neither for the living nor for the dead.

There was never a time when I did not exist, nor you, nor these princes. And there will never come a time when we cease to exist. As the Self passes through this body from childhood to youth and to old age, so does the Self acquire another body after death. A wise person is not perplexed by these changes....

The non-existent can never come to be and the existent can never cease to be. This reality of these two is understood by the seers of the truth. That spirit which pervades the entire universe is indestructible. No one can destroy this unchanging reality. Our physical body must inevitably come to an end, but the eternal, immeasurable embodied Self is indestructible. Therefore, fight, Arjuna!

He who thinks that this Self can kill or that this Self can be killed, fails to perceive the truth. The Self can neither kill nor be killed. The Self was never born and it does not die. Having come to be, it will never cease to be. Birthless, eternal, undecaying, and primordial, this Self does not die when the body dies....

As a man puts on new clothes after discarding old ones, the Self discards old bodies and takes on new ones. Weapons cannot cut it, fire does not burn it, water does not dampen it, and wind does not wither it. It is eternal, all-pervading, changeless and, immoveable. It is called the unmanifested, the unfathomable, and the unchangeable. Since you know this to be the case, why should you grieve?

Even if you think that this Self is perpetually subject to birth and death, even then, Arjuna, you should not grieve. For death is inevitable for the living and birth is inevitable for the dead. Since this cycle is unavoidable, you have no reason for your sorrow...."

The Knowledge of Rebirth [4.1-11]

Krishna said, "I taught this eternal doctrine to Vivasvat. Vivasvat taught it to Manu, and Manu taught it to Ikshvaku. The great sages knew this doctrine, which they handed down from generation to generation. But over time, Arjuna, it has become lost.

Today I have described this same teaching to you, because you are my sincere devotee and friend. It is a profound secret, indeed."

Arjuna said, "You were born long after Vivasvat. How is it possible that you instructed him in this doctrine?"

Krishna said, "You and I have both been reborn many times, Arjuna. The difference is that I remember all of these rebirths, whereas you do not. Although I myself am unborn, eternal, and the Lord of all beings, through my own divine power (*maya*), I manifest myself in various (finite) forms. Whenever there is a decline in righteousness (*dharma*) and disorder runs rampant, then I manifest myself. From time to time, I come into being for the protection of the good, the correction of the wicked, and to reestablish righteousness. He who understands my true nature and works will not be born again when he leaves his body, but becomes one with me. By becoming one with me, many have become freed of attachment, fear, and anger—purified by the fire of knowledge (*jnana tapas*)."

THE PATH OF SELFLESS ACTION

Action and Its Fruits [2.39-41, 47-52]

"I have revealed the wisdom of higher knowledge to you, Arjuna. Now listen to the wisdom of selfless action! By this means will you break free from the bonds of *karma*. On this path, your efforts are never wasted and your gains never reversed. Even a very little of this practice protects one from great sorrow. The thoughts of those who are resolute on this path are single-pointed, but the thoughts of the irresolute wander in numerous directions after many aims....

You have a right to your actions, but not to the fruits of your actions. Don't let the fruits of your actions be your motivation, but don't be enamored by inaction either. Perform your duty without attachments, maintaining your calm in the face of success and failure. This equanimity is called yoga....

The wise perform actions with no thoughts to results, whether good or evil. Therefore focus on right action. For yoga is skill in action. The wise, guided by pure intellect, renounce the fruits of action. Becoming freed of the bondage of rebirth, they attain a state beyond all suffering...."

The Path of Selfless Action: Action and Inaction [3.1-9]

Arjuna asked Krishna, "If you think that the path of knowledge is superior to the path of action, why do you then advise me to engage in this horrible war? Your conflicting words confuse my mind. Therefore please tell me decisively by which means I may attain the supreme good."

Krishna replied, "In this world, I have said, there are two paths that one may follow—the path of knowledge (*jnana yoga*) for those who are contemplative and the path of unselfish action (*karma yoga*) for the active. One does not attain freedom from the bondage of *karma* by merely abstaining from action. One does not attain perfection [in this way], because there is no one who remains actionless even for a moment. Everyone is driven to action necessarily by the forces of nature. Those who abstain from action while allowing their minds to dwell on sense objects are simply pretending. But one who controls his senses through a well-trained mind and works without attachment to results should be considered far superior.

Perform any actions that you are required to do, because action is better than inaction. You couldn't even maintain your body without some sort of action. Unless you act in the spirit of selfless service to others, your actions are a form of enslavement to the world. So make your action a sacrifice and become free of all attachments...."

The Cause of Selfish Action [3.36-42]

Arjuna asked, "Krishna, what is it that causes one to engage in selfish actions, as though these actions were forced and against one's own will?"

Krishna said, "It is desire and aversion, arising from passion. It is all-consuming and taints everything. As fire is covered by smoke, as a mirror by dust, and an embryo by a womb, similarly is self-knowledge obscured by selfish desire, which is mankind's greatest enemy.

This selfish desire is found in the senses, the mind, and the intellect, clouding over the understanding with delusion. Therefore, Arjuna, by regulating your senses, conquer this enemy, the destroyer of knowledge and wisdom.

The senses, they say, are superior to the body, the mind superior to the senses, the intellect superior to the mind, and the Self superior to the intellect. Therefore, knowing what is supreme, allow the Self to subdue your ego, destroying selfish desire—difficult as that might be."

Selfless Action and Liberation [4.19-23]

[Krishna said,] "A person is called wise by the sages when all his undertakings are free from the motive of desire and his deeds are purified by the power of wisdom. By abandoning all thoughts of the fruits of his actions, totally contented and dependent upon nothing, he does nothing even while engaged in all sorts of activity. He does not become attached even while performing actions, being free of expectations and desires and totally self-controlled.

Satisfied with whatever comes along, beyond thoughts of pleasure and pain, free from envy, and the same in success and failure, he remains unbound (by *karma)*. The bonds of one who is without attachment, whose mind is free and established in wisdom, and who does work as a sacrifice are thus dissolved entirely.

The Path of Selfless Action and the Path of Renunciation [5.1-4, 6]

Arjuna said, "Krishna, you have recommended both the path of selfless action and the path of the renunciation of action (*sannyasa*). Please tell me which of these two is the better path."

Krishna replied, "The renunciation of action and the performance of selfless action will both lead to the supreme goal. Of the two, however, selfless action is better.

One who is engaged in true renunciation is beyond duality, affected by neither like nor dislikes, and freed from bondage. Only the ignorant think that (pure) contemplation (*Samkhya*) and action (*yoga*) are different, but the wise know better. One who practices either of these deeply will gain the rewards of both....

The renunciation of action is difficult without engaging in action. But the wise man, following the path of selfless action, soon attains freedom."

The Effects of Selfless Action [5. 7-11, 18-21]

He who follows the path of selfless action, who is pure, who has conquered his senses and ego, has realized his own self as the Self in all. Even while engaged in action, he is not bound by his actions. Understanding this truth, he knows "I am not the doer." Even while seeing, hearing, touching, smelling, eating, walking, sleeping, breathing...; even while speaking, grasping or letting go, opening his eyes and shutting them, he understands that these are simply movements of the senses acting upon sense objects. He who surrenders all selfish attachments is no more tainted by sin than a lotus flower is dampened by water. Renouncing his attachments, one who follows the path of selfless action uses his body, mind, and senses for the sake of self-purification....

One who follows this path. Arjuna, looks upon all beings as equal. He sees the same Self present in a wise priest, a cow, an elephant, a dog, or an outcast. While in the world, he has mastered it, for his mind continually rests in the Absolute (Brahman). He is neither elated when good things happen to him nor depressed when he experiences what is bad. Lucid and serene, his mind is firmly established in the Absolute. Not dependent upon the pleasures of this world, and with his mind purified through spiritual practice, he finds joy in his own Self."

THE PATH OF MEDITATION

The Practice of Meditation [6.11-19, 25-26]

Krishna said, "One aspiring to liberation (i.e., the yogi) should strive constantly to concentrate his mind in meditation on the Supreme Reality, alone, self-controlled, free from desires and possessions.

Sitting down on a firm seat that is neither too high nor too low, on a clean spot that covered with grass, a deerskin and a cloth, he should concentrate his whole mind on a single object. Controlling his thoughts and the activities of his senses, he should practice meditation for self-purification.

Holding his body, head and neck erect and still, he should concentrate upon the tip of his nose, without allowing his eyes to wander. Sitting there, serene and fearless, free of desire, he should mediate upon me and have me as his supreme goal. By keeping his mind always fixed upon me, with his thoughts under control, he will attain peace, the Supreme Nirvana contained within me.

Meditation is not for him who eats too much or too little, who sleeps too much or too little. But for one who is moderate in eating, recreation, working, sleeping, and waking, this yoga of meditation will destroy all sorrow. When the mind becomes free of all desires and is centered upon the Self, then one is said to be well-established in yoga. Just as the flame of a lamp in a sheltered spot is unwavering, so too is the mind of the meditator who practices union with the Self....

Little by little, by controlling the intellect, the mind will become fixed upon the Self alone. Whenever the wavering and unsteady mind of the meditator wanders away, let him gently restrain it and bring it back under the control of the Self...."

The Bliss of Meditation [6.20-22, 27-32]

"When the mind becomes disciplined by the practice of meditation, the meditator sees the Self through the Self, experiencing the joy of the Self. He then experiences the bliss that is perceived only through the purified intellect and which is beyond the realm of the senses. Having experienced this absolute reality, he will never again become separated from it. Attaining this state, he knows that there is no greater good and he becomes established there, where even the greatest sorrows can no longer disturb him....

Supreme bliss comes to the one whose mind has become stilled, whose desires are controlled, who is free from faults, and who has become one with the Absolute. Having mastered himself and put away sin, he experiences the bliss that comes from contact with the Eternal. He who experiences the unity of all life, sees himself in all beings and all beings in himself, and looks upon all with an equal eye. For one who sees me in everything and everything in me, I am never lost, nor is he ever lost to me. One who recognizes the unity of life perceives me in all beings. Whatever his situation in life, he abides in me.

He is a perfect yogi who sees all beings as equal—whether in distress or joy—because they are like himself."

The Difficulties of Meditation [6.33-45]

Arjuna said, "Krishna, I don't see how I can attain the state of equanimity that you've just described, when my mind is so restless. For the mind is fickle, unsteady, turbulent, wild, stubborn—as hard to control as the wind.

Krishna replied, "Arjuna, certainly it is very difficult to control the restless mind, but it is possible through the practice of meditation, with perseverance and detachment. For one whose mind is not subdued, the practice of meditation is difficult, indeed. But one who possess self-control and who follows the right means will succeed."

Arjuna said, "But what happens to that person of faith who, because of a wandering mind, fails to succeed in this practice? Does such an individual, unmoored and bewildered, simply perish like a cloud scattered in the sky, lost both in this world and the hereafter? Krishna, please dispel this doubt of mine, because only you can do it!"

Krishna replied, "There is no destruction for such an individual either in this world or the hereafter. For no evil will befall one who strives to do good. One who has strayed from the yogic path goes to realms of the righteous, where he lives for many years, eventually to be reborn into a pious and prosperous family. Or he may eventually be born into a family of yogis rich in wisdom. Such a birth is rare, indeed, in this world. There he revives the knowledge that he gained in a previous life and works again to achieve perfection. Unconsciously he returns to the practices of his former life....Then, after many lives, the one who strives in this way, whose is free of fault, attains the Supreme Goal of life...."

THE PATH OF DEVOTION

The Divine Manifestations [7.1-10, 16-19, 24-26]

Krishna said, "Listen, Arjuna, and I will tell you how you can come to know me in my full perfection with certainty. I will reveal this wisdom to you and how it may be realized, after the experience of which there will be nothing left for you to know in this world. Only one out of thousands of persons strives for self-realization; and of those, scarcely one among them knows me in truth.

Earth, water, fire, air ether, mind, intelligence, and ego are the eightfold divisions of my manifested nature (*prakriti*). This is my lower nature. But beyond this, Arjuna, is my higher nature, which sustains the entire universe. All beings have their source in these two natures. I am the origin of the entire universe and its dissolution as well. There is nothing higher than me: everything that exists is strung on me like pearls on a thread.

I am the taste of water, the radiance of the sun and moon.

I am the sacred syllable OM in the Vedas, the sound of the ether, and the potency in human beings.

I am the sweet fragrance of the earth, the heat in fire, the life force of all that lives, the austerity of the ascetics.

I am the eternal seed of all that exists.

I am the intelligence of the intelligent, the brilliance of the brilliant....

Those virtuous individuals who come to worship me are of four kinds—the distressed, the seeker of knowledge, the seeker of wealth, and the wise. Of these, the wise man, who is ever united to me and totally devoted to me, is the best. For I am very dear to him and he is very dear to me. All of these types are worthy, but I regard the wise man as my own Self, because he is the one that abides unwaveringly in me. After many lifetimes, the wise man unites with me, knowing me to be the cause of all. Such great souls are rare....

The ignorant assume that I, the Unmanifest, have entered into some form, not knowing that my true nature is changeless and supreme. Veiled by my creative power (*maya*), I do not reveal myself to such, who do not realize that I am unborn and imperishable. Arjuna, I know all beings in the past, present, and the future, but there is no one who knows me completely....."

Revealing the Divine Mystery [9.1-14. 16-34]

Krishna said, "Since you are filled with faith, I will reveal to you the profound mystery, the knowledge of which combined with experience, will liberate you from the all suffering. This supreme, most secret knowledge, purest and best, is most easy to practice and everlasting. Those who lack faith cannot attain me, Arjuna, and must return to the path of birth and death (*samsara*).

The entire universe is pervaded by me through my unmanifest form. All beings are in me, but I am not in them. But in truth these beings do not reside in me. Behold my divine mystery! Although I am the sustainer of all beings, I am not confined by them. Understand that, just as the mighty wind moving everywhere, abides in the sky, in this way all beings abide in me.

At the end of one cosmic cycle, all beings return to my primal material nature and at the beginning of the next, I send them forth again. Under the control of nature (*prakriti*), I project forth multitudes of beings again and again, whether they will it or not. But these acts of mine do not bind me, because I remain serene and unattached. Under my guidance, nature produces all things and thus keeps creation in motion.

The ignorant disregard me when I am clad in human form, unaware that in my higher form I am Lord of all. They are filled with worthless hopes, worthless actions, and worthless knowledge and their lives become frivolous and evil.

But the truly wise, under the protection of my divine nature, are devoted completely to me, knowing that I am the immutable source of all things. Always glorifying me, steadfast in their vows, bowing down before me, they worship me continually with intense devotion....

I am the ritual and the sacrifice.

I am the medicine, the mantra, and the clarified butter.

I am the fire itself and the act of offering.

I am the support of the universe—its father, mother, and grandfather.

I am the object of all knowledge, the purifier, the sacred syllable OM, and the Vedas.

I am the goal, the sustainer, the Lord, the witness, the abode, the refuge, the one true friend.

I am the creation and annihilation, the foundation of all, the resting place, and the eternal seed.

I am the bringer of heat and I am the bringer and withholder of the rain.

I am immortality and I am also death. Both being and non-being are within me.

Those who follow the rituals prescribed in the Vedas, the drinkers of the sacred nectar whose sins are cleansed,...attain the heavenly realm and enjoy celestial pleasures. After their merit is spent, however, they eventually fall back into the mortal realm...to experience birth and death, again and again. But those who worship and meditate upon me constantly, to them I will assure the fulfillment of their aspirations and permanently safeguard that which they attain.

Those who worship other gods, if they do so in faith, also worship me, Arjuna, even if they don't know it. I am the object of all sacrifices, but those that don't know me in my true nature must be reborn. Worshippers of the gods go to the gods, worshippers of the ancestors go to the ancestors, worshippers of spirits go to spirits, but those who worship me will come to me.

If one offers me a leaf, a flower, fruit, or water with love and devotion, I will accept it. O Arjuna, whatever you do, whatever you eat, whatever sacrifices you make, whatever you give away in charity, whatever austerities you perform, do these as an offering to Me. In doing so, you will become freed from bondage to karma and its good and bad results. Then, through the act of renunciation you will be liberated and come to me.

I look upon all equally. I favor none and reject none. But those who worship me with devotion are in me and I am in them.

Even a sinner becomes righteous if he worships me with single-minded devotion. How quickly such a person becomes righteous and attains a last peace. Know this, Arjuna: no one who truly loves me will ever perish. All those who take refuge in me—whatever their station in life—will attain the supreme goal. How much more is this so for brahmins and sages.

Having entered this fleeting and sorrowful world, worship me. With your mind fixed on me, love me, worship me, and serve me. Having disciplined yourself in this way, you will most certainly come to me."

The Divine Powers [10.1-11]

Krishna said, "Arjuna, listen further to my supreme words, which I share for your welfare, since you are so dear to me.

Neither the gods nor the sages know my origins, for I am the source of them all. He who truly knows me as the unborn, the beginningless, Lord of the universe, is freed from all delusion and sin. Understanding, wisdom, truth, self-control, and peacefulness, pleasure and pain, birth and death, fear and fearlessness; nonviolence, equanimity, content, austerity, charity, fame and infamy—all these come forth from me alone.

The seven great sages of old and the four ancient ancestors from whom all human beings descended were born from my mind and came forth from me. He who understands my glorious manifestations and creative power is forever united with me.

I am the origin of all; everything emanates from me. Those who know this truth worship me with intense devotion. Their thoughts are fixed upon me and their lives are totally devoted to me. They derived immense satisfaction from enlightening one another about me.

To those who are constantly devoted to loving and serving me, I give them the understanding whereby they can come to me. Out of mercy, I destroy the ignorance in their hearts through the shining lamp of wisdom."

More of the Divine Manifestations [10.12-16, 19-22, 34, 39-42]

Arjuna said, "You are the supreme Brahman, the highest abode, the ultimate sanctifier, the supreme Self, the source of all, the all-pervading and absolute being. All of the [sages and seers] have proclaimed it so and now you declare this to me yourself. O Krishna, I totally believe everything that you have told me to be true. For neither demigods nor demons can fully understand your real nature. O source of all, master of all, god of gods, Lord of the universe, you alone know yourself by yourself. Please teach me fully of you divine manifestations, by which you pervade these worlds..."

Krisha replied, "Alright, Arjuna, I shall now describe to you the most prominent of my manifestations, for there is no end to them.

I am the Self residing in the hearts of all beings; I am the beginning, middle, and end of all of them.

Of the celestial gods, I am Vishnu; of the lights, I am the radiant sun; of the wind gods, I am Marichi; of the stars, I am the moon.

Of the Vedas, I am the Sama Veda; of the gods, I am Indra; of the organs, I am the mind; in living beings, I am consciousness....

I am death, the destroyer of all, and the source of all things yet to come....

I am the seed of all beings, Arjuna, for without me nothing, animate or inanimate, can exist.

There is no end to my divine manifestations, Arjuna. I have given you only a few illustrations of my infinite glory. Wherever you find strength, grace, or beauty, you may be assured that these have sprung from my splendor.

But what need do you have to know all of this, Arjuna? With a single fragment of my being, I sustain the entire universe."

The Cosmic Vision [11.1-21, 26-34, 43-45, 47-55]

Arjuna said, "Through the instructions concerning the supreme mystery that you have given me, you have cleared up my confusion. You have explained the origin and end of all beings, O Krishna, and have told me of your eternal glories. You have declared yourself to be the Supreme Lord, and I know this to be so. Now I wish to see your cosmic form. If you think it's possible for me to endure it, please show me a vision of your imperishable Self."

Then Krishna said, "Behold, Arjuna, my hundreds and thousands of divine forms in various colors and shapes. Behold all the celestial beings and many wonders never seen before. And here today, behold the whole universe—all things, animate and inanimate—living in me, and anything else you would see. But you cannot see me with the human eye of yours. So I grant you the supernatural sight to behold my divine being."

Having spoken these words, Krishna, the exalted Lord, revealed his universal form to Arjuna. He appeared in this marvelous vision with countless mouths and eyes, with numerous ornaments, and many heavenly weapons. Wearing divine garlands and garments, anointed with heavenly ointments, he showed himself as the resplendent one—wondrous, brilliant, and boundless. If the light of a thousand suns was to blaze forth all at once in the sky, that might begin to resemble the radiance of that exalted being.

In that vision, Arjuna saw the manifold divisions of the entire universe, united in the one supreme Lord.

Filled with wonder, his hairs standing on end, Arjuna bowed with his hands folded before him, and addressed the Lord in this way: "O Lord, I see assembled in your body all the gods and multitudes of beings, as well as Brahman seated on the lotus throne, and all the heavenly sages and serpents. I behold you in infinite form with countless arms, bellies, faces, and eyes, expanding everywhere, limitless. In you, O universal form, I see no beginning, middle, or end. With your crown, scepter, and discuss, you are like a blaze of splendor, difficult to behold, brilliant as the sun, and quite immeasurable.

I believe that you are the changeless, supreme reality to be realized, the ultimate resting place of this universe, the immortal spirit, the guardian of the eternal law (*dharma*). You are [all-encompassing], touching everything with your infinite power. You have countless arms; the sun and the moon are your eyes; your mouth blazes with fire, scorching the entire universe. O Lord, you fill the heavens and earth with your radiance. When this wondrous, terrible form of yours is seen, the celestial spheres tremble with fear. The gods themselves enter into you, filled with awe, their hands folded in prayer. The great hosts of sages and saints sing praises to your glory....

I see the sons of sons of Dhritarashtra, together with the hosts of kings, and those warriors on our side too—all rushing into your fearful mouths. And some I see mangled between your jaws, their heads crushed. As the numerous currents of rivers all flow into the sea, so do these heroes rush into your flaming mouths. As moths fly into the blazing fire to perish there, so do these men pour into your mouth to their own destruction.

O Vishnu, you seem to swallow up entire worlds, burning them with your fiery radiance. Tell me who you are in this terrifying form. Have mercy, O supreme one, let me know you, so that I might better understand you."

Krishna said, "I am death, the destroyer of worlds. I have come here to annihilate all these people. Even without your participation, all these warriors gathered here on the battlefield will die. Therefore, rise up and gain glory; conquer your enemies; enjoy a prosperous kingdom. I have already destroyed these warriors. You are merely my instrument, Arjuna. Therefore, kill them and do not be disturbed. If you fight, you will certainly vanquish your enemies in battle...."

Then Arjuna said, "You are the father of all things, animate and inanimate. You are the ultimate object of worship, and master of all. In the entire universe, there is nothing equal to you, so how can anything be greater than you, O Lord of immeasurable power? Therefore I fall down and prostrate myself before you and seek your blessing. Forgive me the way a father would his son, a friend his true companion, and a lover his beloved. I am delighted to have seen you as you have never been seen before. And yet, my heart is stricken with fear. O Lord, please show me your other more familiar form...."

Krishna said, "Arjuna, by my divine power I have shown you my universal form, luminous and infinite, which no one before you has ever seen. Not by the study of the Vedas, nor by sacrifices, nor by gifts, nor by ceremonial rites, nor by severe austerities has any other being seen what you have seen, Arjuna. Do not be distressed and confused by seeing such a terrible form of mine as this. With a peaceful mind, behold now this earlier form of mine."

After speaking these words, the Lord once again took on the pleasant form of Krishna and consoled the terrified Arjuna.

Arjuna said, "Krishna, seeing this serene human form of yours, my mind is once again calm and returned to normal."

Then Krishna said, "It is extremely difficult for anyone to experience the vision that you just had, which even the gods themselves desire to experience. Not through the Vedas, nor through austerity, nor by gifts, nor even by sacrifice can I be seen in the form in which you have seen me. But through single-minded devotion, I can be known, seen directly, and entered into, Arjuna. He who does every action for my sake, who makes me the supreme goal of his life, who acts without selfish attachment, and who is friendly to every living creature—he attains me."

THE HARMONY OF THE FOUR PATHS

The Four Paths Compared [12.1-12]

Arjuna asked, "Lord, who has the better grasp of yoga: those who are steadfast in their devotion to you or those who worship the impersonal aspect of the Absolute?"

Krishna replied, "Those ever-steadfast devotees of supreme faith who fix their minds on me in worship, I consider most perfect in yoga. But those who worship the immutable, the imperishable, the unmanifest, the impersonal Absolute, with their senses controlled and even-minded in all circumstances, will also come to me. But those who fix their attention on the impersonal, unmanifest Absolute face greater hardships, because comprehension of the unmanifest is difficult for embodied beings. But those who...worship me with unwavering devotion I swiftly deliver from the ocean of life and death. Therefore, focus your mind on me and let your intellect dwell upon me and you will be united with me forever. If, however, you cannot fix your mind steadily upon me, then learn to do so by the practice of meditation. If you're unable to practice meditation, then devote yourself to service for my sake, since this too will lead to the supreme goal. If you are unable to do even this, surrender yourself to me and work to renounce the fruits of all your actions.

Knowledge is superior to blind action and meditation is better than knowledge. But even better is to surrender the fruit of action, since peace will immediately follow....

All Paths Lead to the Supreme Goal [4.11, 13.24-25]

"Whatever way people try to reach me, I accept them; whatever path they may travel, it eventually leads to me."

Some realize the Self within them through meditation, others by knowledge, and still others through selfless service. Again, there are those who are ignorant of these yogic paths, but, hearing from authorities, engage in worship. They too cross beyond death through the practice of devotion."

THE LIFE OF THE LIBERATED

The Man of Steady Wisdom [2.54-72]

Arjuna said, "Krishna, how would you describe the man whose wisdom is steady and who has reached the state of bliss. How does such a man speak? How does he sit? How does he walk?"

Krisha said, "One who is completely freed from all desires of the mind and is satisfied with the Self alone—that is a man of steady wisdom. One whose mind is unperturbed in suffering, who no longer craves pleasure, who is free from lust, fear, and anger, who is freed from selfish attachments, and who is neither elated nor pained when good or bad things happen—that is a man of steady wisdom. One who can completely draw back the senses from sense objects the way a tortoise draws back its limbs into its shell—that is a man of steady wisdom.

The desire for sense pleasures fades if one abstains from sense enjoyment, but the taste for them remains. But even the taste disappears when one has reached the highest goal. Arjuna, the tumultuous senses carry off the mind even of one who strives for perfection. Let him restrain them and keep his mind focused entirely on me. Then he shall stand firm in wisdom.

Attachment to sense objects comes from having the mind fixated on these objects. From attachment comes desire and from desire comes anger. From anger comes delusion, and from delusion confusion of memory. Through confusion of memory, understanding is destroyed. And when understanding is destroyed, ruin follows.

But a man with a disciplined mind, who can move freely among the objects of sense without craving or aversion, will attain perfect peace. When there is such peace, all sorrows are destroyed forever, for the mind of one at peace soon becomes steady.

One who does not have a steady mind cannot concentrate. Without the ability to concentrate, there can be no meditation. Without meditation, there can be no peace. And without peace, how can there be happiness? When the mind constantly follows after the call of the senses, it drives away wisdom, like a storm blowing a ship off course.

Therefore, Arjuna, one who can withdraw himself from the objects of the senses will become established in wisdom. The sage is awake while the world sleeps and, during the time when others are awake, it is night to him. He, whom objects of desire enter as waters flowing into the ocean, which though filled remains tranquil—he alone attains perfect peace. He who abandons all desires, who acts free from craving, without any sense 'I,' 'me,' and 'mine'—he alone attains perfect peace.

One who attains this divine state, Arjuna, even at the moment of death experiences the bliss of God."

The Equanimity of the Liberated [6.7-9]

[Krishna said,] "The Ultimate Reality is manifested in he who has achieved control over his mind and body. When he has mastered himself, a man is perfectly content in heat and cold, in pleasure and pain, in honor and dishonor. For one filled with wisdom and self-realization, a piece of earth, a lump of stone, or fine gold are all the same. He looks with the same impartiality upon friends, family, and enemies, upon those who are neutral towards him, predisposed, or hostile, upon saints and sinners alike."

The One Who is Dear to God [12.13-19]

[Krishna said,] "He who is incapable of hatred towards any being, who is kind and compassionate, free from egoism and pride, the same in the face of pleasure or pain, patient, contented, self-controlled, who is totally dedicated to me, and who is a devotee of mine—that is the one who is dear to me.

He who causes no agitation to anyone and whom no one is capable of agitating, who does not get carried away by joy, anger, fear, or anxiety—that is the one who is dear to me.

He who is beyond expectation, who is pure, diligent, free from all concerns and cares, and who is selfless in his actions—that is the one who is dear to me.

He who neither rejoices nor hates, grieves nor desires, to whom all good and evil fortune is the same—that is the one who is dear to me.

He who treats friends and enemies alike, who is the same with regard to both honor and disgrace, heat and cold, pleasure and pain, who is free from attachments, who disregards praise and blame, who is quiet, content with all, at home everywhere, and full of devotion—that is the one who is dear to me."

PRACTICES

Choosing Your Path

"Whatever way people try to reach Me, I accept them; whatever path they may travel, it eventually leads to Me." (*Bhagavad Gita* 4.11)

One of the remarkable things about Hinduism is the recognition that, just as individuals differ from one another in personality and temperament, so too must there be different spiritual paths for them to follow. As we've seen, while these paths might seem divergent in terms of their philosophies and practice, they are ultimately understood to lead to the same place—to *moksha* or liberation.

Having read the last four chapters on the four yogas—Jnana, Bhakti, Karma, and Raja—and ideally having engaged in some of the spiritual practices connected to these yogas, it's probably the case that one of these paths resonated with you more forcefully than the others. This most likely would have something to do with your particular personality: more philosophical types would naturally gravitate towards Jnana Yoga, emotional types towards Bhakti Yoga, active types towards Karma Yoga, and contemplative types towards Raja Yoga.

So let's start by identifying the particular yogic path that you think is optimal for you and the particular practice(s) within that path that you might consider exploring further:

The yogic path that resonated with me the most was....

The specific practice(s) connected with this path that I would like to explore more fully in the future is/are:

This is a great first step on your road to self-realization. But it's just a first step. A spiritual practice like any other kind of developmental activity—i.e, learning to play a musical instrument or trying to become physically fit—is something that requires consistent effort over a long period of time to master. You wouldn't expect to become a proficient piano player, for example, just by practicing whenever the mood struck you, would you?

Perhaps you've decided that Bhakti Yoga is the optimal path for you and that you'd like to try to do some mantra work in the future. That's terrific, but now you have to actually commit yourself to some kind of regular practice if you want to see any lasting benefits. In general for any spiritual practice to produce benefits, it should be done on a daily basis, at a time when you are most free from distractions. For some people that's probably first thing in the morning after they wake up, but for others it could be immediately upon getting home from work, or possibly right before bed.

When and where will I practice?

One of the best ways to sustain any kind of regular practice—spiritual or otherwise—is to find like-minded individuals who are also committed to the practice. If you're interested in body-building, for example, it is much easier to commit yourself to the workouts required to build up your muscles if you join a local gym and can benefit from the wisdom of those who have been doing this kind of activity for a while.

So explore your own local community to see what kinds of resources are available for group practice. Twenty years ago in the United States, you might have been hard pressed to find a Hindu temple or Buddhist meditation center outside of large cities. Today, these sorts of institutions abound just about everywhere. Just try to find a spiritual community that works best for you.

Where are the places for group spiritual practice in my local community?

If you engage in some form of legitimate spiritual practice over a long enough period of time—and particularly, if you have the support of like-minded practitioners—you should begin to see some definite benefits in your own life. Perhaps you'll find yourself becoming less stressed-out or agitated so easily; or maybe your level of compassion or generosity towards others has increased.

What long-term benefits do I hope to get out of this practice?

GLOSSARY OF HINDU TERMS

advaita	non-dualism, monism.
ahimsa	noninjury, nonviolence.
ananda	bliss.
artha	wealth; social status.
ashrama	a stage of life (e.g., householder).
Atman	the eternal self or soul.
avatar	manifestation or incarnation; the form that a divine being takes to come to earth.
avidya	ignorance.
bhakti	devotion. The *bhakta* is one who follows the path of devotion.
bhakti-marga	spiritual path of devotion, involving loving devotion to one's chosen deity.
Brahma	God as creator.
brahmacari	celibate; stage of life of a student of the Vedas (from twelve to twenty-four).
Brahman	ultimate reality; the eternal, unchanging reality that underlies all things.
brahmin	member of the priestly caste in Hindu society.
chit	consciousness.
dalit	untouchable; one who is outside the caste system.
devas	gods, divine beings.
dharma	duty, law, proper social role.
dvaita	dualism.

gunas	The three qualities that characterize all material phenomenon: sattva, rajas, and tamas.
guru	spiritual master.
Ishta-deva	ones preferred deity.
Isvara	Lord.
jiva	individual self.
jnana	knowledge.
jnana-marga	spiritual path of knowledge, whereby one attains liberation by recognizing the true nature of the Self.
kama	pleasure; sensual pleasure.
karma	moral law of cause and effect pertaining to actions.
karma-marga	spiritual path whereby one acts without concern for the fruits or consequences of one's actions.
kshatriya	members of the warrior caste.
lingam	phallus; symbol for the god Shiva.
mantra(m)	a sacred formula used in prayer or meditation.
maya	illusion that serves to mask the divine.
moksha	"release" from the cycle of rebirth; the goal of spiritual life for most Hindus.
nirguna	without attributes; e.g., Nirguna Brahman.
Om	a sacred syllable in Hinduism, symbolizing the ultimate reality in the universe.
prakriti	the energy out of which the physical world manifests itself.
prana	life-breath.
Purusha	the primordial man or cosmic being in the Vedas. Later, pure spiritual reality (as opposed to *prakriki*).
rajas	the quality of material reality characterized by activity.
rishis	seers; the sages to whom the Vedas were revealed.
rita	the cosmic order ordained by the gods.
sadhu	holy man.
saguna	with attributes; personalized form of the divine; e.g., sarguna Brahman.

samadhi	trance-like state in yoga in which self-consciousness is lost.
samsara	cycle of rebirth or reincarnation.
sannyasin	wandering ascetic; one who has renounced the world.
sat	being.
sattva	the quality of material reality characterized by purity.
shruti	literally, "what is heard."
shudra	lowest of the four classes, made up of servants and laborers.
smriti	literally, "what is remembered."
sukta	Vedic hymn.
tamas	the quality of material reality characterized by darkness / inertia.
vaishya	members of the merchant or artisan class.
varna	social class (e.g., Brahmin, warrior, merchant, serf).
Vedanta	philosophical approach within the jnana-marga (path of knowledge) that holds that all reality is Brahman.
yogi	one who practices yoga.

FOR FURTHER READING

ESSENTIAL PRIMARY SOURCES

The following should be considered essential works for anyone seeking a deeper understanding of the various traditions of Hinduism. Other translations of each of these works can be found, but these are among the most readable contemporary editions:

The Bhagavad Gita. Trans. Eknath Easwaran. Tomales, CA: Nilgiri Press, 2007.

The Law Code of Manu. Trans. Patrick Olivelle. New York: Oxford University Press, 2004.

The Rig Veda. Trans. Wendy Doniger. London: Penguin, 1981.

The Upanishads. Trans. Vernon Katz and Thomas Egenes. New York: Jeremy P. Tarcher, 2015.

The Yoga Sutras of Patanjali. Trans. Edwin F. Bryant. New York: North Point Press, 2009.

PRIMARY SOURCES: ANTHOLOGIES

Doniger, Wendy, ed. *Norton Anthology of World Religions: Hinduism.* New York: W.W. Norton and Co., 2015.

Doniger O'Flaherty, Wendy, ed. *Textual Sources for the Study of Hinduism.* Chicago: University of Chicago Press, 1988.

Embree, Ainslie, ed. *The Hindu Tradition.* New York: Random House, 1966.

Goodall, Dominic, ed. *Hindu Scriptures.* Berkeley: University of California Press, 1996.

Olsen, Carl. *Hindu Primary Sources: A Sectarian Reader.* New Brunswick, NJ: Rutgers University Press, 2007.

INDIAN HISTORY

Basham, A.L. *A Cultural History of India.* Oxford: Oxford University

Press, 1975.
—. *The Wonder that Was India*. New York: Grove Press, 1954.
Keay, John. *India: A History*. New York: Grove Press, 2010.

HINDUISM: GENERAL

Bhaskarananda, Swami. *The Essentials of Hinduism: A Comprehensive Overview of the World's Oldest Religion*. Seattle: Viveka Press, 2002.
Flood, Gavin D. *An Introduction to Hinduism*. Cambridge: Cambridge University Press, 1996.
—. *The Blackwell Companion to Hinduism*. Oxford: Blackwell, 2003.
Fowler, Jeaneane. *Hinduism: Beliefs and Practices*. Brighton, GB: Sussex Academic Press, 1997.
Frazier, Allie M. *Hinduism*. Philadelphia: Westminster Press, 1969.
Klostermaier, Klaus K. *A Survey of Hinduism*. Albany: State University of New York Press, 1989.
Knipe, David M. *Hinduism*. New York: HarperCollins, 1991.
Lipner, Julius. *The Hindus: Their Religious Beliefs and Practices*. New York: Routledge, 1998.
Michaels, Axel. *Hinduism: Past and Present*. Princeton. NJ: Princeton University Press, 2005.
Sen, K.M. *Hinduism*. London: Penguin, 1961.
Sharma, Arvind. *Classical Hindu Thought: An Introduction*. New Delhi: Oxford University Press, 2000.
Zaehner, R.C. *Hinduism*. Oxford: Oxford University Press, 1966.

HINDU PHILOSOPHY (SYSTEMS OF)

Dasgupta, S.N. *History of Indian Philosophy*. Vol. 1. Cambridge: Cambridge University Press, 1957.
Hamilton, Sue. *Indian Philosophy: A Very Short Introduction*. Oxford: Oxford University Press, 2001.
Herman, A.L. *An Introduction to Indian Thought*. Englewood Cliffs, NJ: Prentice-Hall, 1976.
Hiriyanna, M. *Outlines of Indian Philosophy*. Delhi: Motilal Banarsidass, 2009.
Müller, F. Max. *The Six Systems of Indian Philosophy*. New York: Longmans, 1928.
Prabhavananda, Swami. *The Spiritual Heritage of India*. Hollywood, CA: Vedanta Press, 1979.

Raju, P.T. *The Philosophical Traditions of India*. London: George Allen and Unwin, 1971.

Zimmer, Heinrich. *Philosophies of India*. London: Routledge, 1951.

YOGA: GENERAL

Adiswarananda, Swami. *The Four Yogas*. Woodstock, VT: Skylight Paths Publishing, 2006.

DeLuca, Dave. *Pathways to Joy: Master Vivekananda on the Four Yoga Paths to God*. San Francisco: Inner Ocean Publishing, 2003.

Feuerstein, Georg. *Yoga: The Technology of Ecstasy*. Los Angeles: Jeremy P. Tarcher, 1989.

—. *The Yogic Tradition: Its History, Literature, Philosophy and Practice*. Prescott, AZ: Hohm Press, 2001.

Vivekananda. *The Four Yogas*. New York: SophiaOmni Press, 2017.

THE VEDAS AND VEDIC INDIA

Bloomefield, Maurice. *The Religion of the Vedas*. G.P. Putnam and Sons. New York, 1908.

Meta, P.D. *Early Indian Religious Thought*. London: Luzac and Co., 1959.

Monier-William, Monier. *Brahmanism and Hinduism*. 4th ed. New York: Macmillan and Co., 1891.

JNANA YOGA

General

Marchand, Peter. *The Yoga of Truth*. Rochester, VT: Destiny Books, 2007.

Vivekananda, Swami. "Jnana Yoga." *The Four Yogas*. New York: Sophia Omni, 2017.

The Upanishads

Deussen, Paul. *The Philosophy of the Upanishads*. Edinburgh: T & T Clark, 1908.

Keith, Arthur Berriedale. *The Religion and Philosophy of the Veda and Upanishads*. 2 Vols. Cambridge: Harvard University Press, 1925.

Vedanta

Hodgkinson, Brian. *The Essence of Vedanta*. Royston, GB: Eagle Editions: 2006
Swartz, James. *The Essence of Enlightenment: Vedanta, The Science of Consciousness*. Boulder, CO: Sentient Publications, 2014.
Torwestern, Hans. *Vedanta: The Heart of Hinduism*. New York: Grove Press, 1991.
Vrajaprana, Pravrajika. *Vedanta: A Simple Introduction*. Vedanta Press, 1999.

BHAKTI YOGA

General

Radhnath, Swami. *The Journey Within: Exploring the Path of Bhakti*. San Rafael, CA: Mandala Publishing, 2016.
Ram Dass. *Be Here Now*. Lama Foundation, 1971.
Steven Knapp. *Bhakti Yoga Handbook*. Detroit, MI: World Relief Network, 2013.
Vivekananda, Swami. "Bhakti Yoga." *The Four Yogas*. New York: SophiaOmni, 2017.

Mantra Practice

Ashley-Farrand, Thomas. *Healing Mantras*. New York: Ballentine, 2008.
Easwaran, Eknath. *The Mantram Handbook*. Tomales, CA. Nilgiri Press, 2008.
Frawley, David. *Mantra Yoga and the Primal Sound*. Twin Lakes, WI: Lotus Press, 2010.
Radha, Swami Sivananda. *Mantras: Words of Power*. Spokane, WA: Timesless Books, 2011.

KARMA YOGA

Sivananda, Swami. *Practice of Karma Yoga*. Uttaranchal, India: Divine Life Society, 1995.
Vivekananda, Swami. "Karma Yoga." *The Four Yogas*. New York: Sophia Omni, 2017.

RAJA/ASHTANGA YOGA

General

Cope, Stephen. *The Wisdom of Yoga*. New York: Bantam, 2007.

Eliade, Mircea. *Yoga: Immortality and Freedom*. Princeton: Princeton University Press, 2009.

Farhi, Donna. *Yoga Mind, Body and Spirit*. New York: Henry Holt, 2000.

Feuerstein, Georg. *The Yoga Tradition: Its History, Literature, Philosophy, and Practice*. Prescott, AZ: Hohm Press, 1998).

——. *Yoga: The Technology of Ecstasy*. Los Angeles: J.P. Tarcher, 1989.

Kriyananda, Swami. *The Art and Science of Raja Yoga*. Crystal Clarity Publishers, 2011.

Maehle, Gregor. *Ashtanga Yoga: Practice and Philosophy*. New World Library, 2007.

Rama, Swami. *The Royal Path: Practical Lessons on Yoga*. Honesdale, PA: Himalayan Institute Press, 1996.

Sturgess, Stephen. *The Supreme Art and Science of Raja and Kriya Yoga*. London: Singing Dragon, 2015.

Vivekananda, Swami. "Raja Yoga." *The Four Yogas*. New York: Sophia Omni, 2017.

The Yoga Sutras

Bachman, Nicolai. *The Path of the Yoga Sutras*. Boulder, CO: Sounds True, 2011.

Sarbacker, Stuart Ray and Kimple, Kevin. *The Eight Limbs of Yoga*. New York: North Point Press, 2015.

Thakar, Vimala. *Glimpses of Raja Yoga: An Introduction to Patanjali's Yoga Sutras*. Berkeley, CA: Rodmel Press, 2005.

Whicher, Ian. *Integrity of the Yoga Darsana*. Albany: State University of New York Press, 1998.

Pranayama

Brown, Richard P. and Gerbang, Patricia L. *The Healing Power of the Breath*. Boston, MA: Shambhala, 2012.

Brule, Dan. *Just Breathe*. New York: Simon and Schuster, 2017.

Iyengar, B.K.S. *Light on Pranayama*. London: George Allen and Unwin, 1983.

Maehle, Gregor. Innaloo City, WA: Kaivalya Publications, 2012.

Rama, Swami, et al. *The Science of Breath*. Himalayan Institute, 2007.

Richard Rosen. *Pranayama: Beyond the Fundamentals*. Boston: Shambhala, 2006.

—. *The Yoga of Breath*. Boston: Shambhala, 2002.

THE BHAGAVAD GITA

Dasa, Bhurijana. *"Surrender Unto Me": An Overview of the Bhagavad Gita*. Vrindavan, India: VIHE Publishing, 1997.

Easwaran, Eknath. *The Bhagavad Gita for Daily Living*. 3 Vols. Tomales, CA: Nilgiri Press, 2003.

Gandhi, Mohandas K. *The Bhagavad Gita According to Gandhi*. Berkeley, CA: Berkeley Hills Books, 2000.

Ram Dass. *Paths to God: Living the Bhagavad Gita*. New York: Harmony Books, 2004.

Rosen, Steven J. *Krishna's Song: A New Look at the Bhagavad Gita*. Westport, CT: Praeger, 2007.

Made in the USA
Middletown, DE
04 September 2021

46683618R00116